The Jenny Craig™ COOKBOOK

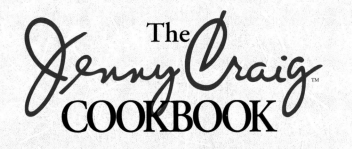

The Jenny Craig COOKBOOK

CUTTING through the FAT

Oxmoor House®

Library of Congress Catalog Card Number: 95-71179
ISBN: 0-8487-1496-2

Manufactured in the United States of America
Fourth Printing 1996

Be sure to check with your health-care provider before making any changes in your diet.

Editor-in-Chief: Nancy Fitzpatrick Wyatt
Senior Foods Editor: Katherine M. Eakin
Senior Editor, Editorial Services: Olivia Kindig Wells
Art Director: James Boone

The Jenny Craig™ Cookbook

Editor: Cathy A. Wesler, R.D.
Designer: Melissa Jones Clark
Copy Editor: Shari K. Wimberly
Editorial Assistants: Valorie J. Cooper, Stacey Geary
Contributing Editors: Jan Strode, Lisa Talamini Jones, R.D.
Contributing Writer: Pamela B. Haskell
Director, Test Kitchens: Kathleen Royal Phillips
Assistant Director, Test Kitchens: Gayle Hays Sadler
Test Kitchen Home Economists: Molly Baldwin, Susan Hall
    Bellows, Julie Christopher, Iris Crawley, Michele Brown Fuller,
    Natalie E. King, Elizabeth Tyler Luckett, Jan A. Smith
Senior Photographer: Jim Bathie
Photographers: Ralph Anderson, Van Chaplin, Gary Clark,
    Tina Evans, Beth Maynor, Howard L. Puckett,
    Charles Walton IV
Senior Photo Stylist: Kay E. Clarke
Photo Stylists: Virginia R. Cravens, Cindy Manning Barr,
    Marjorie Johnston, Cathy Muir
Publishing Systems Administrator: Rick Tucker
Production and Distribution Director: Phillip Lee
Associate Production Manager: Theresa L. Beste
Production Assistant: Valerie Heard, Marianne Jordan Wilson

Cover: *Mocha Fudge Pie (page 110), Citrus-Mint Cooler (page 80), Shrimp Alfredo (page 162), Bruschetta with Basil (page 56), Grilled Pepper and Squash (page 195)*

Dedication

⁓

I dedicate this book to my mother, Gertrude Guidroz,
who insisted I learn how to cook and for being the
best teacher a daughter could ask for. And to everyone who
pursues healthy living as a way of life.

Contents

Dear Readers,

Thirty-five years and 45 pounds ago, I began a journey that would change my life forever and eventually touch the lives of millions. It was at the request of many of these people that we created this first ever Jenny Craig cookbook.

For years, people have asked me for weight management tips and for recipes that are low in fat and calories, and big on taste. They wanted recipes that I would eat to stay healthy and fit. People also wanted help with all the confusing and often conflicting information that is out there today.

My hope is to share with you, in the pages of this book, the motivations and inspirations that have helped me most along the way and to share, from my own perspective, about how our quality of life is directly proportional to the quality of our choices. You'll discover that healthy weight management is not about making sacrifices—it's about making smart choices for yourself.

My personal journey started after the birth of my second child, Michelle. It was during that pregnancy that I gained an additional 45 pounds. When I looked at myself in the mirror, I was presented with the stark reality that I had to make a change. With deep-down determination, I resolved to lose the weight. The choice took commitment, but it remains one of the most important decisions I've ever made.

Now at age 63, and a grandmother of seven, I feel great and lead an active and full life. I attribute my good health to the choice I made years ago to make nutrition and exercise an integral part of my life. A healthful lifestyle has become a habit for me. I eat what I want because I've learned over time to cook and eat the right things. You too can learn how to prepare great-tasting low-fat, low-calorie foods and how to make exercise an ingredient of choice.

In this book I hope you'll find, as I did, a new respect for balance and moderation in the foods you eat and in the physical demands you make on your body. With this balance will come a natural beauty, regardless of age, that will radiate from the inside out.

Keeping pace with new trends in exercise and nutrition can be confusing, but this book literally slices through all the information circulating about rights and wrongs, do's and don'ts. We'll give it to you straight—and in a practical way.

In *The Jenny Craig Cookbook* you'll find 180 recipes that have been tested, lightened, and nutritionally perfected for you in the test kitchens of Oxmoor

House, Inc. Cooking and eating great-tasting healthy foods has become a
passion for me. Sharing that passion with others has become my mission.

I want to thank you, my readers, and clients at our Jenny Craig Centres
for your encouragement and support in making this book possible. I hope it
will help you enjoy your life's journey as much as I've enjoyed mine. Remember
to eat well and exercise. Make it a habit. And have fun!

Jenny Craig

Living Light & Loving It

Living Light & Loving It

You've heard of the benefits of healthy eating and moderate exercise, most notably increased longevity. And that's incentive enough to reduce fat and cholesterol intake and to increase physical activity.

But it's the prospect of a livelier and more rewarding life that really makes "taking control" an exciting adventure. Exciting because you alone can make changes in the way you feel today and, more remarkably, the way you'll feel ten years from now.

But what about the time it'll take to plan and prepare the meals, let alone exercise sessions? Don't worry. In this cookbook, you'll find quick, healthy recipes and menus ready to prepare. And we've given you tips to trim the fat while achieving maximum flavor. Plus, you'll see how physical activity, especially something fun, can easily slip right into your busy day once you know a few tricks.

Are you too tired to cook because of a hectic schedule? Until now, maybe driving to a take-out window or ordering a pizza has been your solution for a quick meal. But wait. Healthy foods can be just as fast. All it takes is some basic information, and your desire to eat for good health.

That's what this book is all about—preparing delicious low-fat food quickly and easily, giving you extra time to enjoy all of the other things in your life.

To start you on your way, turn to page 24 for ways to trim fat and calories from recipes while still attaining great-tasting results. And we'll walk you through the grocery store, beginning on page 20, with key tips for selecting foods low in fat but brimming with essential nutrients.

Nutrition Know-How

It's not hard to figure out what's good for you when it comes to basic nutrition: fresh fruits, vegetables, whole grains, the leanest cuts of meat, the dairy products lowest in fat. And it usually takes little effort to highlight these foods at a meal.

The Jenny Craig Food Group Pyramid developed for clients in our Centres helps illustrate the appropriate balance of food in your diet, making it easier than ever to plan healthy meals. Similar to the USDA pyramid, it communicates the same message: Eat less fat, and build your diet upon a base of complex carbohydrates. All foods are represented in the pyramid, emphasizing that you don't have to eliminate your favorites.

When selecting foods, try to:
• increase intake of foods rich in carbohydrates, such as grains, fruits, and vegetables
• eat a moderate amount of protein foods, such as milk, meat, poultry, and fish
• minimize the number of foods high in fat or containing large amounts of sugar

The pyramid is designed to simplify eating. The idea is to "eat low." Plan your daily menu around lean choices from the bottom and middle of the pyramid, balanced by moderate amounts of higher fat foods.

Because there are no bad foods, you can work your favorites—including a dessert or snack—into your menus. Just let balance, variety, and moderation guide your choices.

Balance means eating foods from all the groups and trading off between high- and low-fat foods over the course of several days.

Variety means choosing from all the groups, as well as eating different foods within each group—apples and oranges, broccoli and carrots, fish and chicken—to get the spectrum of nutrients you need daily.

Moderation means that you don't eliminate—just moderate. There's room for all foods, in reasonable amounts, in a low-fat lifestyle.

Fat and Oil exchange

Milk exchange

Meat exchange

Fruit exchange

Vegetable exchange

Grain exchange

Jenny Craig Food Group Pyramid

The Skinny on Fats

If "low fat" is good for your health, is "no fat" better? Not necessarily. Our bodies need some fat to survive. Fat has these important functions:
- carrying and storing the fat-soluble vitamins (A, D, E, and K) in the body
- helping maintain the function of cell membranes
- cushioning and protecting vital body organs
- maintaining hormonal balance

From a taste standpoint, fat carries a food's flavor, and it makes you feel satisfied at the end of a meal. Again, moderation is key. If you could make only one nutritional change in your eating habits, most experts agree that reducing fat intake should be your goal.

Currently, people in the United States consume about 37 percent of their calories each day from fat, well over our recommended 20 to 30 percent guideline. Some of it comes from obvious sources such as butter, margarine, and vegetable oils. Other fats aren't so visible. They're hidden in luncheon meats, snack foods, and bakery items such as cakes, cookies, pies, and pastries.

Take a look at the type of fat that you consume. Some fats are healthier than others. Here are some tips on choosing which ones to include in your diet:
- Stay away from **saturated fats** found in coconut, palm, and palm kernel oils—they have been found to contribute to heart disease.
- Go for the heart-healthy **monounsaturated fats** in peanut, almond, walnut, canola, avocado, and olive oils, which may help lower blood cholesterol levels.
- **Polyunsaturated fat**, found in vegetable oils like corn, soybean, safflower, sunflower, canola, and cottonseed oils, may help reduce blood cholesterol when used in place of saturated fats.

The all-purpose polyunsaturated oils are mild-flavored, moderately priced, and great for salad dressings, baked goods, and light sautés. The monounsaturated oils are a bit pricier, but a little goes a long way. Olive oil adds depth to Italian, Mexican, and Greek fare. Hot sesame oil gives a bite to an Oriental stir-fry. The delicate flavors of avocado oil and walnut oil are ideal for salad dressings and baked goods. Canola is the best of both worlds—it's mild and moderately priced.

How Much Fat Do You Need?

Fats should make up no more than 20 to 30 percent of your total calories, and most of us eat more fat than we think. Everything from salad dressings to packaged rice pilaf can be loaded with fat calories that sneak into your meals when you think you're eating healthy. Here are two methods to help you keep an eye on fat intake.

Fat Exchanges
If you're accustomed to using food exchanges, simply track your fat allowance by counting fat exchanges. Your daily meal plan can include the number of exchanges according to your calorie level.

Fat Gram Budget—Easy as 1, 2, 3
To easily keep track of the fat you're eating, keep a fat gram budget. Instead of calculating fat percentages for individual foods, translate the 20 percent into grams of total fat for the day and set this as your fat budget. Your fat budget should be based on the calories you're consuming.

Fat Exchange Allowance

Calorie per Day	Fat Exchanges*
1,200	2
1,500	3
1,800	4
2,000	5
2,200	6

* Based on 20% of calories from fat.

1. Figure out how many calories your body requires. To do this, multiply your current weight by 13 if you're a female or by 15 if you're a male. This is a rough estimate because calorie requirements vary depending on gender, age, body size, and activity level. For weight loss, subtract 500 calories per day to allow for a loss of 1 pound of body fat a week. A diet of less than 1,000 calories a day, however, isn't recommended unless medically supervised.

Setting Your Daily Fat Budget		
Calories	Calories from Fat*	Fat Grams†
1,200	240	27
1,500	300	33
1,800	360	40
2,000	400	44
2,200	440	49

*Calories from fat are 20 percent of total calories.
†Fat grams are calories from fat divided by 9.

2. Determine your fat allowance. Refer to the *Setting Your Daily Fat Budget* chart (at left) to determine the amount of fat grams allowed each day for you to stay within the recommended percentage. For example, if you're consuming 1,500 calories per day, you should eat no more than 33 grams of fat per day to stay within the 20 percent guideline. If your calorie level isn't listed, calculate your fat allowance by multiplying your calorie requirement by 30 and dividing by 9. (Fat contains 9 calories per gram.)

3. Monitor your fat balance by subtracting the fat grams that you consume.

Vitamins and Minerals

Vitamins and minerals are essential to good health. Small amounts of a wide variety are required each day. Ideally, a single "health" food would provide them all, but unfortunately no such food exists. Consuming a variety of food is the best way to include adequate amounts of all the essential nutrients, especially vitamins and minerals.

Researchers are linking certain vitamins to cancer prevention. The attention-getters are vitamins A, C, E, and folic acid.

Vitamins and Minerals for Your Health	
Nutrient	Source
Vitamin A	Liver; eggs; cheese; fortified milk; fruits; and yellow, orange, and dark green vegetables (carrots, broccoli, spinach)
Vitamin C	Citrus fruits and juices; tomatoes; strawberries; melons; green peppers; potatoes; dark green vegetables
Vitamin E	Vegetable oils; margarine; wheat germ; whole-grain breads and cereals; liver; dried beans; green leafy vegetables
Folic Acid	Liver; dark green, leafy vegetables; wheat germ; dried beans and peas; orange juice; cantaloupe
Calcium	Milk and milk products; sardines and canned salmon (eaten with bones); dark green, leafy vegetables; dried beans and peas

Calcium deficiency is associated with osteoporosis, a severe loss of bone density that threatens older adults. The recommended daily allowance for calcium is 800 milligrams a day for men and women. Pregnant and lactating women are advised to consume 1,200 milligrams daily.

Exercise Your Options

Healthy eating is just part of the lifestyle equation. You've got to factor in exercise as well. And if you think that means hours of grueling workouts in a stuffy gym, it's not true!

There's great news—the concept of exercise is changing. Fitness experts say that just moderate amounts of physical activity are enough to reap tremendous health benefits. And that's especially encouraging as exercise is one of the major factors in maintaining weight loss.

Exercise also strengthens bones and muscles. You may find that you're sleeping better and feeling less stressed once you incorporate physical activity into your lifestyle.

So start exercising by gradually increasing your daily activity. You'll find that squeezing fitness into your already busy schedule isn't as hard as you think. Just seize any opportunity to move around—try taking the stairs, parking far away, walking instead of driving your kids to school (they need the exercise too!), and trading coffee breaks for walk breaks.

The key to exercise is to "accumulate." Every bit of physical activity counts, like gardening, cleaning house, and walking to the grocery store.

If you don't have time for a 30-minute workout, walk three times for 10 minutes each time. You can burn the same number of calories, lose weight, and maintain good health. As you build a naturally active lifestyle, slowly add more exercise over time. Go at your own pace and think about how good you feel!

For the Health of It

Get active . . . and see what moderate exercise can do for you!

- Reduces risk of heart attack
- Lowers blood pressure
- Reduces body fat
- Improves muscle tone
- Increases flexibility
- Increases self-confidence
- Decreases risk of developing diabetes
- Lessens symptoms of menopause
- Reduces stress
- Decreases risk of cancer
- Increases bone strength
- Strengthens heart and lungs
- Improves sleep
- Increases energy level

Be Active

Tennis

Dancing

Biking

Hiking

Gardening

Sailing

Berry picking

Bowling

Canoeing

In-line skating

Kite flying

Seashell hunting

Snowman building

Get moving, have fun! Choose an activity that you enjoy and then think of

Attitude Adjustment

People who lose weight and keep it off know the difference between **weight loss** and **weight management**. Weight loss is just dieting down to a goal, but weight management is learning how to maintain that goal forever. It isn't just a one-shot deal—it's a lifelong commitment that takes a change in attitude.

The best way to get started is just that—GET STARTED. Take small steps, not big leaps, at first. Start by weaving small changes into the way you shop, cook, and exercise. Weight is a reflection of lifestyle—change your lifestyle, and the weight will follow.

Be sure to **think success**! Focus on your accomplishments, learn from your lapses, and strive for improvement, not perfection. Avoid vowing to "always" or to "never" do something. Instead, expect to succeed. A positive attitude will keep you headed toward a healthier life.

Getting Started

Refer to these pointers from time to time, and you'll be on your way to the lifestyle you've always wanted:

• Set realistic goals. A mere 10 percent decrease in your weight can make all the difference in your well-being.
• Go for a moderately reduced-calorie, low-fat menu. Don't try to lose too much too fast; instead, aim for slow, steady weight loss. One to two pounds a week is safe and realistic.
• Don't be extreme, be consistent. Commit to the long haul and make small changes that will become part of your lifestyle.
• Plan ahead. This helps you avoid high-risk emotional/social situations that might distract you from your goals.
• Make exercise, not food, your first choice for stress release. Get outside, get active, and get moving—you'll feel the stress slip away.
• Surround yourself with people who support your mission.
• Exercise regularly. It's the key to managing your weight over the long term.
• Reward yourself. Learning to give yourself even the smallest reward encourages you to continue along the path to good health.

it as play. Remember, it's never too late to get started.

Streamline Your Shopping

The first step to easy *and* healthy cooking is knowing how to shop. Here are some tips on staples that build the foundation for quick, nutritious meals.

For fast food preparation, buy ingredients in the closest to usable form. This means choosing such items as skinned, boned chicken breasts, shredded cheese, and bags of prewashed salad greens. You may pay a little more, but if you have very little time to cook, then the cost is small compared to high-fat fast-food fare.

Breads, Grains, and Cereals

Many markets carry a variety of breads, cereals, and grains, so it's easier than ever to get creative. Experiment with different kinds of rice and beans, and boost your nutrition quotient for the day while spicing up the dinner table. Complex carbohydrates—as supplied by whole grain breads and cereals, fruits, vegetables, and vegetable proteins—come with an added bonus: dietary fiber.

The National Cancer Institute recommends eating 25 to 35 grams of fiber each day to reduce the risk of heart disease, cancer, obesity, and diabetes. Most Americans need to double their present fiber intake to reach this goal. So as you select carbohydrate foods, remember that the more unprocessed or unrefined a food is, the more fiber it contains.

Your daily bread—Bread is basically low in fat. It's what you smear on that bagel that packs the fat and calories. French bread, bagels, whole-grain bread, pita bread, and tortillas are low-fat choices (check labels for 2 grams of fiber and less than 3 grams of fat). Treat yourself only occasionally to higher fat choices like croissants, muffins, pastries, and biscuits.

Crack the cracker myth—Many crackers are loaded with fat and sodium. Look for those with less than 3 grams of fat per serving, and keep an eye out for your favorite brand in a reduced-fat version. Watch portions though. It's easy to load up on calories while popping bite-sized bits into your mouth.

Cereal sense—Choose cereals that don't list sugar as the first ingredient. Whole grains like oats, whole wheat, and rice are the best bets, and keep a sharp eye on oil content.

Great grains—With the amazing assortment of grains on the market these days, you can include bulgur, oats, quinoa, and others in your diet for added fiber, vitamins, and taste. For packaged grain dishes, look for reduced-fat or reduced-salt versions.

Pasta power—The number of pasta varieties is surpassed only by the number of ways to prepare it. From angel hair to ziti, fresh or dried, plain or flavored, there's a pasta to tantalize your taste buds. Rich sauces, not the pasta itself, contain the calories and fat.

Beautiful beans—Beans are a low-fat powerhouse of carbohydrates, protein, iron, and fiber. Most beans are available in cans or jars, so they're ideal for quick meals.

Produce Picks

You can get most of the nutrients your body needs in the produce section. So build your diet around fresh fruits and vegetables and you can't go wrong. Reach for what's in season for the best flavor and price, like juicy peaches, plump tomatoes, and sweet corn in the summer. Vary your fruit and vegetable choices to include the collage of nutritious items available today.

Fresh fruits are great choices for both nutritional and economical value. Many stores carry cut fruit for easy snacking and toss-together salads. Again, purchase what's in season. Unsweetened frozen fruits and those canned in their own juices are also good choices. Whole fruits are a better choice than fruit juice because they take longer to eat and provide fiber and fullness.

Fiber Facts

Each of these foods are good sources of fiber and contain less than 100 calories.

1 to 4 grams dietary fiber
1 slice whole wheat bread
1 slice cracked wheat bread
1 slice seven-grain bread
1 cup fresh cauliflower flowerets
1 cup fresh spinach
½ cup legumes (beans, lentils, peas)
½ cup seedless grapes

5 to 10 grams dietary fiber
½ cup 100% bran cereal
¼ cup 40% bran flakes cereal
1 cup cooked broccoli
3 medium carrots
1 medium apple, unpeeled
1 medium pear, unpeeled

Bone Up on Calcium

Your mom was right when she said "Drink your milk!" Unfortunately, you're probably not consuming enough dairy products to get the calcium you need.

To reduce the possibility of osteoporosis, women aged 25 and older need 1,000 milligrams a day. Women who are post-menopausal and who aren't on estrogen need 1,000 to 1,500 milligrams daily. Eat low-fat dairy products and leafy green vegetables, and consider a calcium supplement. And don't forget the workouts—weight-bearing exercise is another protective measure against osteoporosis.

If you do buy juice, choose those that are 100% juice. Each day, try to eat at least one fruit high in vitamin C. Instead of the usual citrus, consider cantaloupe, strawberries, kiwifruit, mango, or papaya. In a hurry? Buy sliced, assorted fruit from your market's deli section, or keep a pop-top four-pack of individually portioned applesauce, peaches, or fruit cocktail on hand.

Crunchy, colorful vegetables are menu builders. Fresh, frozen, or canned vegetables (in that order) boast nutrients from vitamin A to zinc. Visit your supermarket's salad bar, where you may be able to find broccoli flowerets ready to steam or stir-fry, greens ready for tossing, melons and pineapple already cut up, and other short-cut produce. In the produce section, you may find vegetables that are already chopped and washed for maximum convenience, so go for the greens! Plan fun vegetarian meals from time to time, and no one will miss the meat.

From the Dairy

Stick to **nonfat dairy products**, including skim milk, nonfat yogurt, and fat-free or low-fat cottage cheese, to get essential protein, calcium, and vitamins without extra cholesterol and fat. Plain nonfat yogurt makes a great alternative to sour cream or oil in recipes. Choose yogurts with 90 calories or less and at least 200 milligrams of calcium per serving.

Cheese lovers who think they need to avoid cheese because of saturated fat and cholesterol can turn to reduced-fat cheeses, which have a protein and fat content similar to lean meat. Select varieties that have less than 5 grams of fat per ounce, like part-skim mozzarella and Jarlsberg lite.

From the Meat Counter

Red meat in and of itself isn't fattening. Rather it's the cut that determines fat content. For lower fat choices, stick to cuts that are labeled "leg" and "loin" and remove all visible fat. The leanest of the lean includes leg and loin of veal, pork loin and ham, leg of lamb, and beef loin, sirloin, and top/bottom/eye of round. When it come to quick and convenient, think small cuts and pieces: steaks, chops, scallops, fillets, tenders, boneless breasts, shish kabobs, tenderloins, and ground.

Pick poultry! It's one of the lowest fat meats around, so stock up on breast cuts of both chicken and turkey. Choose white or breast meat and remove the skin. Try ground chicken or turkey in place of ground beef, but remember that regular ground turkey can have as much fat as regular ground beef. Look for ground turkey breast for the leanest choice.

Most fish are low in fat, and they all cook quickly. Some of the lower fat varieties include cod, flounder, haddock, halibut, shellfish, and water-packed tuna.

Less Fat, More Flavor

Making meal-by-meal adjustments is the best approach to changing your diet, especially when you're trying to decrease fat intake. With our recipes you'll find that low fat and good flavor are not mutually exclusive terms. Adding flavor without adding fat doesn't require sophisticated culinary skills, only a little knowledge of how to make the most of the natural flavors of foods.

Aside from being lower in fat, what's an added bonus of using the "light touch" when it comes to cooking? More good-for-you nutrients. The rule to remember: The shorter the cooking time for fruits and vegetables, the fewer the nutrients you'll lose during the cooking process. Stir-frying and steaming are quick methods that seal in vitamins and minerals rather than letting them escape into the cooking liquid. Nonstick cookware is ideal for stir-frying, and if you don't have a steamer, you can use an aluminum or stainless steel colander set in saucepan over an inch or two of water. Other techniques to keep the nutrients high and fat low include:

• Grill or broil meats on a rack so that fat drains away, and be sure to trim all visible fat before cooking. As you remove the skin from chicken, also remove the whitish fat pads beneath the skin.

• As you add more fish to your diet, you'll reap the benefits of its rich nutrients. And at about 10 minutes per inch of thickness, its quick cooking time is a real plus.

• When a recipe calls for wine, remember that the flavor remains intact during the cooking while the alcohol evaporates and calories are reduced.

• Jazz up low-fat dishes with flavor enhancers such as citrus juices, flavored vinegars, wine, and apple cider. Each of these liquids are acidic in nature and can accentuate the taste of everything from soups to casseroles to vegetables and entrées. For example, adding a splash of lemon juice to a pan of sautéed carrots takes the flavor from bland to more complex. Sprinkling a fresh or dried herb such as dill on those same carrots adds a second layer to that flavor complexity. In fact, liberal use of herbs is another culinary secret. Learning to cook with herbs and spices opens a whole new horizon of tastes. Can you really change the way you cook without sacrificing your favorite foods? Absolutely!

Fat-Friendly Ways To Cook

Low-fat food doesn't have to be bland. Here are some ways
to cut fat and still treat your tastebuds.

Bake it—Oven baking is the no muss, no fuss way to cook. Use a shallow, uncovered pan and an oven temperature of 350° or higher. You'll find that marinating meat before cooking keeps it moist.

Brown and drain—Brown ground meat and poultry in a nonstick skillet coated with vegetable cooking spray and drain fat drippings using a colander or paper towels.

Sauté it—You can sauté using water, broth, juice, or wine or using a skillet coated with cooking spray. Chop food into bite-sized pieces for quick cooking.

The steam team—Elaborate Chinese stacking bamboo baskets or simple aluminum folding baskets keep food suspended over boiling water to steam fish and vegetables to perfect tenderness.

Chill out—Remove stocks, soups, and stews from the heat, and let cool slightly. Add a few ice cubes, and the fat will congeal around the ice, making it easy to discard the fat.

Grill it—Grilling is a sure-fire way to boost the flavor of meats and vegetables without added fat. Coat the grill rack with cooking spray to keep food from sticking. If your grill is charcoal-fired, try mesquite chips for a smoky flavor.

Rack it up—Roast meats and poultry on a rack coated with cooking spray. For chicken that's breaded, cooking on the rack of a broiler pan allows air to circulate, creating a crisp crust over the entire surface of the chicken.

Wok the talk—A wok used to be for adventurous cooks only, but now many are finding that it is great for low-fat and quick cooking. Just toss chopped vegetables and meats in a little sesame oil and stir-fry your way to healthy eating.

Taste Is King

It's the seasonings—the herbs and spices—that transform a recipe from plain to exotic. A sprig of basil, a dash of vanilla, a bay leaf stimulates, soothes, and intrigues your palate. Be creative but remember a little goes a long way. So start with a pinch, then taste and go from there.

Cumin has a strong pungent flavor and is one of the main ingredients of curry powder. It's used in a wide variety of dishes in Indian, Middle Eastern, and African cuisines.

Ginger has a hot, spicy-sweet flavor and is a mainstay of Oriental and Indian cooking. It's used minced or grated in marinades and sauces, ground in cookies, and crystallized in candies and desserts.

Nutmeg is a dried, oval-shaped seed with a sweet, spicy, slightly bitter flavor. It's used ground or freshly grated in eggnog, warm beverages, fruits, puddings, cakes, breads, and custards.

Peppercorns are available in green (fresh, unripe berries), black (dried green berries), white (dried cores of red berries), and mixed. They have a pungent flavor and are available whole, cracked, or ground.

Red pepper is from the dried fruit of the capsicum pepper plant and has no relation to peppercorns. It has a hot, pungent flavor and is used in sausage, pizza, and Mexican food.

Saffron has a distinctive aroma and a bitter, highly aromatic flavor. It's used to add flavor and bright yellow color to rice, chicken and seafood dishes, soups, and sauces.

To the Table

You're hungry, but what's for dinner? Before you get stressed out trying to answer that question, take a look in this cookbook.

Our recipes use familiar ingredients that you probably already have on hand. After selecting the recipe you want to prepare, scan it to make sure you have everything you'll need.

You will find a few ingredients listed as optional—this means the recipe will be fine without the ingredient but would be extra-special if you included it. For example, Summer Fruit Salad in Lemonade Glaze (page 166) lists Bibb lettuce leaves as optional. If you desire, you can serve the salad on the greens.

Don't Forget the Garnish

No matter how attractive the food is, you'll probably want to add garnishes for special occasions. Garnishes can be as simple as a lining of leafy greens under a salad, or a few sprigs of parsley or other fresh herb on top of a casserole. For more elaborate garnishes, try these:

Carrot Curls—Scrape young, tender carrots, and trim off the top stalk end. Use a vegetable peeler to cut the carrots into paper-thin strips. (If the strips are too thick, they will not roll.) Roll strips up tightly, and secure with wooden picks. Place in ice water, and chill until set. Remove picks before garnishing. Use carrot curls to garnish salads, dips, or meat platters. A sprig of fresh dillweed is a colorful addition to this garnish.

Chocolate Curls—Pour melted chocolate onto a baking sheet lined with wax paper, spreading into a 2- or 3-inch-wide strip. Let stand until the chocolate feels cool and slightly sticky, but not firm. Slowly pull a vegetable peeler across the length of chocolate until a curl forms, letting the chocolate curl up on top of the peeler. Use a wooden pick to transfer the curl to a plate. Chill the curls until ready to use as garnish for cakes, pies, or other desserts.

Citrus Cartwheels—Select firm lemons, limes, or oranges with thick rinds. Holding the fruit firmly in one hand, cut evenly spaced grooves from tip to tip, using a citrus stripper. Cut the fruit crosswise into thin slices. To garnish beverages, make a cut from the outside edge of the slice to the center, and place the cartwheel on the rim of a glass, or float several in a punch bowl filled with fruit punch or in a pitcher of lemonade.

Citrus Strips—Select firm lemons, limes, and oranges with thick rinds. Hold the fruit firmly in one hand, and run a citrus stripper or citrus zester around the outer rind of the fruit to create continuous strips. For curly strips, wrap long strips around the handle of a wooden spoon; cover tightly, and freeze until ready to use. Use a single citrus strip or a bunch to garnish desserts.

Citrus Twists—Cut thin slices from lemons, limes, or oranges. Place each slice on a flat surface, and make a cut to, but not through, the center of the slice. Hold the cut edges of the slice, and twist in opposite directions. Citrus twists are used to garnish almost any dish, particularly seafood or desserts.

Green Onion Fans—Wash green onions, and trim off some of the green tops. Cut off the white end of the onion. Using a sharp knife, snip the ends and branches of the onion into thin strips. Place in a bowl of cold water for a few seconds to curl the ends. The longer the fans remain in the water, the tighter the curl. For tightly curled fans, use ice water. Use to garnish salads, Oriental dishes, or meat platters.

Strawberry Fans—Using firm, ripe strawberries, place each strawberry, green top down, on a cutting surface, and make cuts in the berry, being careful not to slice all the way through. Gently fan out the slices. Strawberry fans are a popular garnish for desserts or cakes, but they also give first courses and salads a special touch.

Tomato Roses—A sharp paring knife and firm, ripe tomatoes are necessary for making tomato roses. Starting at the base of the tomato, trim a paper-thin strip of peel, ¾-inch wide, from the entire tomato. Coil the strip tightly, with the fleshy side inward. When almost all the skin has been rolled, set the tomato rose on its base, and curl the last piece of the skin around to form the open petals. Tomato roses are a nice garnish for a vegetable accompaniment or a meat platter.

Menus

Dinner's almost ready . . .

In planning these menus, we took into consideration that people lead busy lives, and that, as a result, less and less time can be spent in the kitchen preparing food—nutritious or otherwise. With this time factor in mind, we developed menus that are quick and easy, using convenience products where appropriate and giving suggestions on how to prepare the meal in the most efficient way.

At times, you may choose to follow each menu as it's presented, using the photographs to glean ideas for subtleties of presentation—table settings, center-pieces, garnishes—the touches that will make your meals superlatively appealing as well as healthful. And because time is a factor for all of us, use the "Meal Plan" for step-by-step guidance in getting the meal on the table promptly.

Simple Dinners menus begin on page 31 . . .

•*Sunset Supper (page 36)* ushers in the evening with casual simplicity, yet is brimming with flavor and appeal.

•*Drop by for Dinner (page 39)* can save the day when unexpected company suddenly appears. You'll take *them* by surprise when, in just minutes, a mouth-watering meal is ready.

•*Dinner on the Bayou (page 44)* offers low-fat versions of etouffée and bread pudding—two favorites of Louisiana cuisine.

Quick Entertaining menus begin on page 47 . . .

•*Rustic Italian Lunch (page 52)* packs in flavor with herbs you'll have on hand. And your friends will find it hard to believe that rich-tasting Amaretto Velvet Frosty contains less than 1 gram of fat per serving.

•*Dinner for Your Sweetheart (page 55)* is elegant but easy enough to prepare after a busy day at work.

•*An Evening in Japan (page 62)* takes you and your friends on a culinary trip to the Orient.

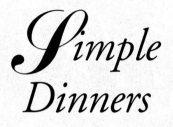

Simple Dinners

Dinner on the Bayou (page 44)

Supper from the Garden Cheddar-Potato Frittata

Garden Greens with Red Pepper Dressing   Zucchini-Orange Bread

Melon with Sweet Onion Dressing

Serves 6   Total calories per serving: 357

Cheddar-Potato Frittata

1½ cups coarsely chopped round red potato
    Vegetable cooking spray
1   cup chopped tomato
¼   cup chopped green onions
½   teaspoon pepper
¼   teaspoon salt
1½ cups frozen egg substitute, thawed
½   cup (2 ounces) shredded reduced-fat sharp Cheddar cheese

Per Serving:
Carbohydrate 10.5g
Protein 10.1g
Fat 2.1g
Fiber 1.4g
Cholesterol 6mg
Sodium 263mg
Calcium 115mg
Exchanges
½ Grain
1 Lean Meat

1 Cook potato in a saucepan in boiling water to cover 10 to 12 minutes or until tender. Drain well.

2 Coat a large nonstick skillet with cooking spray; place over medium-high heat until hot. Add potato, tomato, and next 3 ingredients; sauté until onion is tender.

3 Pour egg substitute over vegetable mixture. Cover; cook over medium-low heat 15 minutes or until set. Sprinkle with cheese. Cover; cook 2 minutes or until cheese melts. Cut into 6 wedges, and serve immediately.

Yield: 6 servings (100 calories per serving).

Garden Greens with Red Pepper Dressing

Per Serving:
Carbohydrate 5.0g
Protein 1.2g
Fat 1.9g
Fiber 1.8g
Cholesterol 0mg
Sodium 106mg
Calcium 26mg
Exchange
1 Vegetable

1   (7-ounce) jar roasted red peppers in water
3   tablespoons white wine vinegar
2   tablespoons water
2   teaspoons olive oil
¼   teaspoon salt
⅛   teaspoon ground red pepper
1   tablespoon minced fresh basil
2   cups torn red leaf lettuce
2   cups torn green leaf lettuce
2   cups torn romaine lettuce
1   cup chopped tomato
1   cup chopped cucumber

1 Drain peppers, reserving liquid. Place half of peppers in container of an electric blender. Reserve remaining peppers and liquid for another use.

2 Add vinegar and next 4 ingredients to blender container. Cover and process until mixture is smooth; transfer to a small bowl. Stir in basil. Cover and chill.

3 Combine lettuces, tomato, and cucumber in a large bowl; toss gently. Arrange evenly on salad plates. Spoon red pepper mixture over salads.

Yield: 6 (1-cup) servings (38 calories per serving).

Zucchini-Orange Bread

Per Slice:
Carbohydrate 18.1g
Protein 2.1g
Fat 1.9g
Fiber 0.4g
Cholesterol 0mg
Sodium 45mg
Calcium 48mg
Exchange
1 Grain

1   cup finely shredded zucchini
1¾   cups all-purpose flour
2½   teaspoons baking powder
¼   teaspoon salt
½   cup sugar
1   teaspoon grated orange rind
½   cup unsweetened orange juice
⅓   cup frozen egg substitute, thawed
2   tablespoons vegetable oil
½   teaspoon orange extract
Vegetable cooking spray

1 Press zucchini between paper towels to remove excess moisture. Combine zucchini, flour, and next 4 ingredients in a large bowl.

2 Combine orange juice and next 3 ingredients, stirring well. Add to dry ingredients, stirring just until dry ingredients are moistened.

3 Spoon batter into an 8½- x 4½- x 3-inch loafpan coated with cooking spray. Bake at 375° for 40 to 45 minutes or until a wooden pick inserted in center comes out clean. Let cool in pan 10 minutes; remove from pan, and let cool completely on a wire rack.

Yield: 16 (½-inch) slices (98 calories per slice).

Melon with Sweet Onion Dressing

2	cups cantaloupe balls
2	cups honeydew melon balls
2	cups watermelon balls
¼	cup sugar
¼	cup unsweetened orange juice
1	tablespoon minced onion
2	teaspoons vegetable oil
¾	teaspoon poppy seeds
¼	teaspoon salt
¼	teaspoon dry mustard

Per Serving:
Carbohydrate 25.8g
Protein 1.5g
Fat 2.3g
Fiber 1.8g
Cholesterol 0mg
Sodium 112mg
Calcium 27mg
Exchanges
1½ Fruit
½ Fat

1 Place melon balls in a large bowl.

2 Combine sugar and remaining ingredients in a small jar; cover tightly, and shake vigorously. Pour over melon balls, and toss gently. Cover and chill. Toss gently before serving. Serve with a slotted spoon.

Yield: 6 (1-cup) servings (121 calories per serving).

"For a jump-start on melon balls, head to your supermarket's salad bar, where you can find melons cut up, ready to toss with Sweet Onion Dressing."— Jenny

Sunset Supper   Turkey Jalapeño

Seasoned Vermicelli and Rice   Snow Pea Stir-Fry

Serves 4   Total calories per serving: 545

• Complete steps 1 and 2 of Turkey Jalapeño; set aside.
• Make Seasoned Vermicelli and Rice; keep warm.
• Make Snow Pea Stir-Fry; keep warm.
• Complete steps 3 and 4 of Turkey Jalapeño.

Supper on the table in 53 minutes

Turkey Jalapeño

1	pound turkey breast cutlets
⅓	cup all-purpose flour
½	teaspoon freshly ground pepper
2	teaspoons vegetable oil
	Vegetable cooking spray
¼	cup sliced green onions
½	teaspoon peeled, minced gingerroot
½	cup red jalapeño jelly
¼	cup unsweetened apple juice
1	tablespoon red wine vinegar
1	teaspoon low-sodium Worcestershire sauce
2	teaspoons cornstarch
1	tablespoon water

Per Serving:
Carbohydrate 38.3g
Protein 31.3g
Fat 5.9g
Fiber 0.7g
Cholesterol 70mg
Sodium 84mg
Calcium 29mg
Exchanges
2 Grain
4 Lean Meat

1 Place cutlets between 2 sheets of heavy-duty plastic wrap; flatten to ⅛-inch thickness, using a meat mallet or rolling pin. Combine flour and pepper; dredge turkey cutlets in flour mixture.

2 Heat oil in a large nonstick skillet over medium heat until hot. Add cutlets, and cook 3 to 4 minutes on each side or until done. Transfer to a platter, and keep warm. Wipe drippings from skillet with a paper towel.

3 Coat skillet with cooking spray; place over medium-high heat until hot. Add green onions and gingerroot; sauté until tender. Add jelly and next 3 ingredients. Reduce heat; cook until jelly melts and mixture is thoroughly heated.

4 Combine cornstarch and water; stir until smooth. Add to jelly mixture. Cook, stirring constantly, until thickened and bubbly. Spoon over turkey.

Yield: 4 servings (335 calories per serving).

Seasoned Vermicelli and Rice

Per Serving:
Carbohydrate 27.0g
Protein 3.5g
Fat 2.2g
Fiber 0.9g
Cholesterol 0mg
Sodium 382mg
Calcium 17mg
Exchanges
2 Grain

1½	teaspoons margarine
½	cup chopped onion
½	cup instant long-grain rice, uncooked
2	ounces vermicelli, uncooked and broken into 1-inch pieces
1¼	cups water
1	(4-ounce) can sliced mushrooms, drained
1½	teaspoons chicken-flavored bouillon granules
½	teaspoon dried oregano
½	teaspoon dried thyme
⅛	teaspoon freshly ground pepper
2	tablespoons chopped fresh parsley

1 Melt margarine in a saucepan over medium-high heat. Add onion, and sauté until tender. Add rice and vermicelli; sauté 3 minutes or until lightly browned.

2 Combine water and next 5 ingredients. Add to rice mixture, stirring well. Bring to a boil; cover, reduce heat, and simmer 10 minutes or until rice and pasta are tender and liquid is absorbed. Fluff with a fork, and stir in parsley.

Yield: 4 (½-cup) servings (141 calories per serving).

Snow Pea Stir-Fry

Per Serving:
Carbohydrate 10.4g
Protein 3.4g
Fat 1.7g
Fiber 2.9g
Cholesterol 0mg
Sodium 100mg
Calcium 42mg
Exchange
1 Vegetable

	Vegetable cooking spray
1	teaspoon dark sesame oil
½	cup diagonally sliced carrot
2	(6-ounce) packages frozen snow pea pods
¼	cup sliced water chestnuts
½	cup canned low-sodium chicken broth, undiluted
2	teaspoons low-sodium soy sauce
1	teaspoon cornstarch

1 Coat a nonstick skillet with cooking spray; add oil. Place over medium-high heat until hot. Add carrot; sauté 2 minutes. Add snow peas, water chestnuts, and broth; bring to a boil. Cover and cook 2 minutes or until crisp-tender.

2 Combine soy sauce and cornstarch; add to vegetable mixture. Cook over medium heat, stirring constantly, until thickened.

Yield: 4 (½-cup) servings (69 calories per serving).

Drop by for Dinner

Oven-Barbecued Pork

Sautéed Kale and White Beans   Cornmeal Drop Biscuits

Pineapple Mint Julep Sundaes   Orange Spice Tea

Serves 6   Total calories per serving: 579

- Prepare Oven-Barbecued Pork.
- While pork bakes, prepare biscuits.
- Prepare Orange Spice Tea.
- Prepare Sautéed Kale and White Beans.
- Prepare Pineapple Mint Julep Sundaes.

Dinner on the table in 45 minutes

Oven-Barbecued Pork

Per Serving:
Carbohydrate 2.5g
Protein 24.5g
Fat 4.3g
Fiber 0g
Cholesterol 79mg
Sodium 113mg
Calcium 9mg
Exchanges
3 Lean Meat

2	(¾-pound) pork tenderloins
	Vegetable cooking spray
2½	tablespoons no-salt-added ketchup
1½	tablespoons cider vinegar
1	tablespoon reduced-calorie maple syrup
2	teaspoons Dijon mustard
1	teaspoon low-sodium Worcestershire sauce
⅛	teaspoon ground red pepper
	Fresh rosemary sprigs (optional)

1 Trim fat from tenderloins. Place tenderloins on a rack in a roasting pan coated with cooking spray. Combine ketchup and next 5 ingredients; brush over tenderloins. Insert a meat thermometer into thickest part of tenderloin, if desired.

2 Bake, uncovered, at 400° for 30 minutes or until meat thermometer registers 160°, basting with remaining ketchup mixture. Let stand 10 minutes; slice diagonally across grain into thin slices. Garnish with rosemary sprigs, if desired.

Yield: 6 servings (152 calories per serving).

Sautéed Kale and White Beans

Vegetable cooking spray
1   medium onion, sliced and separated into rings
3½ cups chopped kale (about 5 ounces)
¼   cup water
1   cup canned cannellini beans, drained
½   cup chopped plum tomato
½   teaspoon dried rosemary, crushed
⅛   teaspoon salt

1 Coat a nonstick skillet with cooking spray; place over medium-high heat until hot. Add onion; sauté 5 minutes. Add kale and water; cover, reduce heat, and simmer 8 minutes or until kale is wilted, stirring frequently.

2 Add beans and remaining ingredients. Cook, uncovered, over medium heat until thoroughly heated.

Yield: 6 (½-cup) servings (51 calories per serving).

Per Serving:
Carbohydrate 9.5g
Protein 2.6g
Fat 0.5g
Fiber 1.7g
Cholesterol 0mg
Sodium 113mg
Calcium 38mg
Exchanges
2 Vegetable

Cornmeal Drop Biscuits

1¼ cups all-purpose flour
⅓   cup yellow cornmeal
1½ teaspoons baking powder
¼   teaspoon salt
¼   cup chopped green onions
¼   teaspoon garlic powder
⅛   teaspoon ground red pepper
¼   cup plus 2 tablespoons skim milk
2   tablespoons vegetable oil
1   tablespoon honey
1   egg, lightly beaten
Vegetable cooking spray

1 Combine first 7 ingredients in a bowl; make a well in center of mixture. Combine milk, oil, honey, and egg; add to dry ingredients. Stir until moistened.

2 Drop by heaping tablespoonfuls, 2 inches apart, onto baking sheets coated with cooking spray. Bake at 400° for 10 to 12 minutes or until lightly browned.

Yield: 1 dozen (98 calories each).

Per Biscuit:
Carbohydrate 15.1g
Protein 2.5g
Fat 3.0g
Fiber 0.6g
Cholesterol 19mg
Sodium 97mg
Calcium 40mg
Exchange
1 Grain

Pineapple Mint Julep Sundaes

Pineapple Mint Julep Sundaes

Per Serving:
Carbohydrate 27.9g
Protein 3.6g
Fat 0.1g
Fiber 0.3g
Cholesterol 0mg
Sodium 59mg
Calcium 135mg
Exchanges
1 Fruit
½ Skim Milk

¾   cup unsweetened pineapple juice
1   tablespoon cornstarch
3   tablespoons bourbon
1   (8-ounce) can crushed pineapple in juice, drained
1   tablespoon minced fresh mint
3   cups vanilla nonfat frozen yogurt
     Fresh mint sprigs (optional)

1 Combine pineapple juice and cornstarch in a small saucepan, stirring until smooth. Stir in bourbon, and cook over medium heat, stirring constantly, until mixture is thickened. Stir in pineapple and minced mint; cook until thoroughly heated.

2 Scoop ½ cup frozen yogurt into each dessert dish; top with pineapple mixture. Garnish with mint sprigs, if desired. Serve immediately.

Yield: 6 servings (121 calories per serving).

Orange Spice Tea

¾   **cup unsweetened orange juice**
⅓   **cup sugar**
8   **orange spice-flavored tea bags**
2   **(3-inch) sticks cinnamon**
5½ **cups boiling water**

Per Serving:
Carbohydrate 14.9g
Protein 0.2g
Fat 0.0g
Fiber 0.1g
Cholesterol 0mg
Sodium 7mg
Calcium 3mg
Exchange
1 Fruit

1 Combine first 4 ingredients in a large pitcher. Add boiling water; cover and steep 10 minutes. Remove and discard tea bags and cinnamon sticks; let cool. Serve over ice.

Yield: 6 (1-cup) servings (59 calories per serving).

Get Psyched!

Without being really motivated to make changes toward a healthier lifestyle, you probably won't. For success, try this exercise: Focus on a goal, like managing your weight. Close your eyes and imagine yourself achieving that goal, and how it feels—the power and confidence it instillls in you. Keep visualizing your goal scene and bringing up those feelings. Then put yourself in a variety of situations, like attending your class reunion, grocery shopping, and even pumping gas. In every situation feel those wonderful feelings. The positive energy will help motivate you to make changes.

Dinner on the Bayou   Crawfish Etouffée

Steamed Rice   Marinated Green Bean Salad   Bread Pudding

Serves 8   Total calories per serving: 575

44

Crawfish Etouffée

⅔ cup all-purpose flour
3   tablespoons vegetable oil
¾ cup chopped onion
¾ cup chopped celery
½ cup chopped green pepper
3   cloves garlic, minced
¼ cup plus 2 tablespoons no-salt-added tomato paste
2   (14¼-ounce) cans no-salt-added chicken broth
1½ pounds cooked, peeled crawfish tails
2   bay leaves
¾ teaspoon ground red pepper
½ teaspoon salt
⅔ cup chopped green onions
¼ cup chopped fresh parsley

Per Serving:
Carbohydrate 12.8g
Protein 23.2g
Fat 7.4g
Fiber 1.3g
Cholesterol 151mg
Sodium 281mg
Calcium 53mg
Exchanges
1 Grain
3 Lean Meat

1 Combine flour and oil in a Dutch oven; cook over medium heat, stirring constantly, until flour is very brown. (Mixture will be dry.)

2 Add onion and next 4 ingredients; stir well. Cook, stirring constantly, 3 minutes. (Mixture will be dry.)

3 Gradually add chicken broth, stirring constantly. Add crawfish and next 3 ingredients. Cook over medium heat 10 minutes, stirring occasionally. Stir in green onions and parsley; cover and let stand 5 minutes. Remove and discard bay leaves.

Yield: 8 (1-cup) servings (214 calories per serving).

Marinated Green Bean Salad

Per Serving:
Carbohydrate 8.9g
Protein 1.8g
Fat 0.3g
Fiber 2.1g
Cholesterol 0mg
Sodium 117mg
Calcium 39mg
Exchange
1 Vegetable

1	pound fresh green beans
16	cherry tomatoes, halved
1/3	cup water
1/3	cup white wine vinegar
3/4	teaspoon dill seeds
1/2	teaspoon sugar
1/2	teaspoon dried crushed red pepper
1/4	teaspoon salt
2	cloves garlic, sliced

1 Arrange beans in a vegetable steamer over boiling water. Cover; steam 3 minutes. Plunge into ice water; drain. Combine beans and tomatoes in a dish.

2 Bring water and vinegar to a boil in a saucepan. Add dill seeds and remaining ingredients. Pour over beans. Cover and marinate in refrigerator at least 8 hours.

Yield: 8 (1/2-cup) servings (38 calories per serving).

Bread Pudding

Per Serving:
Carbohydrate 41.9g
Protein 8.8g
Fat 2.2g
Fiber 1.7g
Cholesterol 58mg
Sodium 212mg
Calcium 189mg
Exchanges
1 Fruit
1 1/2 Grain
1/2 Skim Milk

6	(1-ounce) slices whole wheat bread, toasted and cut into 1-inch pieces
	Vegetable cooking spray
2	eggs
2	egg whites
2/3	cup instant nonfat dry milk powder
1/2	cup sugar
1/2	cup granulated sugar substitute
1/4	teaspoon ground nutmeg
1/4	teaspoon ground cinnamon
1/2	teaspoon vanilla extract
2	cups water
1/2	cup raisins
1	cup chopped fresh peaches

1 Place bread in a 2-quart casserole coated with cooking spray. Combine eggs and next 8 ingredients. Add raisins and peaches; stir gently. Pour over bread. Place casserole in a shallow pan; add hot water to pan to depth of 1 inch. Bake at 325° for 1 hour or until a knife inserted in center comes out clean.

Yield: 8 servings (215 calories per serving).

Quick
Entertaining

Gather in the Garden (page 48)

Gather in the Garden
Poached Salmon with

Cucumber-Dill Sauce   Sugar Snap Peas and Hearts of Palm Salad

Commercial Dinner Rolls   Raspberry Swirl Angel Food Cake

Serves 6   Total calories per serving: 497

Meal Plan for Gather in the Garden

- Make Raspberry Swirl Angel Food Cake.
- Prepare Poached Salmon with Cucumber-Dill Sauce.
- Prepare Sugar Snap Peas and Hearts of Palm Salad.

Dinner on the table in 60 minutes

Poached Salmon with Cucumber-Dill Sauce

2	cups dry white wine
2	cups water
½	teaspoon chicken-flavored bouillon granules
6	peppercorns
4	sprigs fresh dillweed
2	bay leaves
1	stalk celery, chopped
1	small lemon, sliced
6	(4-ounce) salmon fillets (½ inch thick)
	Cucumber-Dill Sauce

Per Serving:
Carbohydrate 2.5g
Protein 25.9g
Fat 9.8g
Fiber 0.1g
Cholesterol 77mg
Sodium 121mg
Calcium 47mg
Exchanges
3 Medium-Fat Meat

1 Combine first 8 ingredients in a skillet. Bring to a boil; cover, reduce heat, and simmer 10 minutes. Add fillets; cook 10 minutes or until fish flakes easily when tested with a fork. Transfer fillets to a platter, using a slotted spoon; cover and chill thoroughly. Discard liquid remaining in skillet.

2 To serve, spoon Cucumber-Dill Sauce over fillets.

Yield: 6 servings (217 calories per serving).

Cucumber-Dill Sauce

⅓	cup peeled, seeded, and finely chopped cucumber
⅓	cup nonfat sour cream
⅓	cup plain nonfat yogurt
2	teaspoons chopped fresh dillweed
1	teaspoon Dijon mustard

1 Combine all ingredients in a bowl, stirring well. Cover and chill thoroughly.
Yield: 1 cup.

Sugar Snap Peas and Hearts of Palm Salad

Per Serving:
Carbohydrate 11.3g
Protein 1.3g
Fat 1.6g
Fiber 0.9g
Cholesterol 0mg
Sodium 5mg
Calcium 15mg
Exchanges
2 Vegetable

1   cup fresh Sugar Snap peas
2   cups torn Boston lettuce
2   cups torn romaine lettuce
1   cup sliced canned hearts of palm, drained
¼   cup sliced green onions
    Honey-Orange Vinaigrette

1 Arrange peas in a vegetable steamer over boiling water. Cover and steam 1 minute or until peas are crisp-tender. Set aside, and let cool.

2 Combine peas, Boston lettuce, and next 3 ingredients in a large bowl; toss well. Pour Honey-Orange Vinaigrette over lettuce mixture; toss gently.

Yield: 6 (1-cup) servings (59 calories per serving).

Honey-Orange Vinaigrette

2   tablespoons cider vinegar
2   tablespoons unsweetened orange juice
1   tablespoon honey
2   teaspoons vegetable oil
⅛   teaspoon onion powder
⅛   teaspoon ground red pepper

1 Combine all ingredients in a small bowl, stirring well with a wire whisk.
Yield: ¼ cup.

Did You Know?

Hearts of palm are the edible inner portion of the stem of the cabbage palm tree. Hearts of palm resemble white asparagus (without the tip), and their taste is similar to that of an artichoke.

Raspberry Swirl Angel Food Cake

½ (10½-ounce) package frozen unsweetened raspberries, thawed
1 cup plus 1 tablespoon water, divided
1 (16-ounce) package angel food cake mix
   Fresh raspberries (optional)
   Fresh mint sprigs (optional)

1 Position knife blade in food processor bowl; add thawed raspberries, and process until smooth. Place raspberry puree in a wire-mesh strainer over a bowl; press with back of spoon against the sides of the strainer to squeeze out juice. Discard pulp and seeds. Place ¼ cup raspberry puree in a small bowl. Reserve remaining puree for another use. Add ¼ cup plus 2½ tablespoons water to ¼ cup raspberry puree; stir well.

2 Place half of egg white powder packet from cake mix in a large bowl; add raspberry-water mixture. Beat at low speed of an electric mixer until combined; beat at high speed until stiff peaks form. Sprinkle half of flour packet from cake mix over raspberry-egg white mixture. Fold into raspberry-egg white mixture.

3 Place remaining egg white powder in a large bowl; add remaining ½ cup plus 2½ tablespoons water. Beat at low speed until blended; beat at high speed until stiff peaks form. Sprinkle remaining half of flour packet over beaten egg white mixture; fold into egg white mixture.

4 Spoon half of raspberry cake mixture into an ungreased 10-inch tube pan; top with half of plain cake mixture. Repeat layers, using remaining raspberry cake and plain cake mixtures. Gently swirl batters with a knife. Bake at 375° for 40 minutes or until cake springs back when lightly touched. Remove cake from oven; invert pan, and cool completely. Loosen cake from sides of pan, using a narrow metal spatula; remove from pan. If desired, garnish with fresh raspberries and mint sprigs.

Yield: 12 servings (149 calories per serving).

Per Serving:
Carbohydrate 34.2g
Protein 3.2g
Fat 0.1g
Fiber 0.9g
Cholesterol 0mg
Sodium 72mg
Calcium 42mg
Exchanges
1 Grain
1 Fruit

Rustic Italian Lunch   Italian Pasta and Bean Soup

Sage and Cheese Biscuits   Amaretto Velvet Frosty

Serves 8   Total calories per serving: 506

Meal Plan for Rustic Italian Lunch

• Complete steps 1 and 2 of Italian Pasta and Bean Soup.
• Make Sage and Cheese Biscuits; keep warm.
• Add pasta in step 3 of soup.
• While pasta cooks, make Amaretto Velvet Frosty.
• Sprinkle cheese over soup.

Lunch on the table in 45 minutes

Italian Pasta and Bean Soup

Vegetable cooking spray
1   tablespoon olive oil
1   cup chopped onion
1   cup sliced carrot
½   cup chopped green pepper
2   cloves garlic, crushed
2   (13¾-ounce) cans no-salt-added beef broth
1   (28-ounce) can crushed tomatoes
1   (15-ounce) can white kidney beans or cannellini beans, rinsed and
      drained
1   (15-ounce) can red kidney beans, rinsed and drained
1½ teaspoons dried Italian seasoning
½   teaspoon salt
½   teaspoon liquid red pepper seasoning
½   teaspoon pepper
6   ounces ditalini pasta
½   cup freshly grated Parmesan cheese

Per Serving:
Carbohydrate 36.2g
Protein 10.8g
Fat 4.5g
Fiber 4.2g
Cholesterol 5mg
Sodium 497mg
Calcium 153mg
Exchanges
2 Grain
1 Vegetable
1 Lean Meat

1 Coat a Dutch oven with cooking spray; add oil and place over medium-high heat. Add onion and next 3 ingredients; sauté until vegetables are crisp-tender.

2 Add beef broth and next 7 ingredients; bring to a boil. Reduce heat to low; cover and simmer 20 minutes, stirring occasionally.

3 Add pasta to vegetable mixture. Cover and cook 10 to 15 minutes or until pasta is tender. Ladle soup into individual bowls; top each serving with 1 tablespoon cheese.

Yield: 8 (1¼-cup) servings (232 calories per serving).

Sage and Cheese Biscuits

Per Biscuit:
Carbohydrate 14.1g
Protein 3.0g
Fat 3.4g
Fiber 0.5g
Cholesterol 2mg
Sodium 130mg
Calcium 101mg
Exchange
1 Grain

1	cup all-purpose flour
1½	teaspoons baking powder
¼	teaspoon salt
1	teaspoon ground sage
½	teaspoon sugar
⅛	teaspoon freshly ground pepper
2	tablespoons margarine
¼	cup plus 2 tablespoons evaporated skimmed milk
2	tablespoons (½ ounce) shredded reduced-fat Monterey Jack cheese

1 Combine first 6 ingredients in a bowl; cut in margarine with a pastry blender until mixture resembles coarse meal. Add milk and cheese; stir just moistened.

2 Sprinkle 1½ teaspoons flour evenly over work surface. Turn dough out onto lightly floured surface, and knead 10 to 12 times. Roll dough to ½-inch thickness; cut into rounds using a 2-inch biscuit cutter. Place on an ungreased baking sheet. Bake at 450° for 8 to 10 minutes or until biscuits are golden.

Yield: 8 biscuits (99 calories each).

Amaretto Velvet Frosty

Per Serving:
Carbohydrate 25.3g
Protein 6.2g
Fat 0.7g
Fiber 0.1g
Cholesterol 2mg
Sodium 97mg
Calcium 222mg
Exchanges
1 Grain
1 Skim Milk

2	cups skim milk
¼	cup instant nonfat dry milk powder
¾	cup amaretto
3	cups vanilla nonfat yogurt
¼	teaspoon vanilla extract
⅛	teaspoon almond extract
	Ice cubes
1	tablespoon chopped almonds, toasted

1 Combine skim milk and nonfat dry milk powder; stir well. Add amaretto and next 3 ingredients. Place half of milk mixture in container of an electric blender.

2 Add enough ice cubes to bring mixture to a 4-cup level; cover and process until smooth. Pour into a large pitcher. Repeat procedure with remaining milk mixture. Sprinkle each serving with almonds. Serve immediately.

Yield: 8 (1-cup) servings (175 calories each).

Dinner for Your Sweetheart

Bruschetta with Basil   Vegetable-Cheese Linguine   Strawberry Sparkler

Serves 2   Total calories per serving: 505

Bruschetta with Basil

Per Serving:
Carbohydrate 14.9g
Protein 5.0g
Fat 3.3g
Fiber 0.7g
Cholesterol 9mg
Sodium 298mg
Calcium 83mg
Exchanges
1 Grain
½ Fat

2 (¾-ounce) slices Italian bread
½ teaspoon olive oil
1 tablespoon nonfat cream cheese product
½ ounce goat cheese
2 teaspoons grated Parmesan cheese
1 (7-ounce) jar roasted red peppers in water
2 small fresh basil sprigs

1 Place bread slices on an ungreased baking sheet; brush evenly with olive oil. Bake at 450° for 5 minutes or until lightly browned.

2 Combine cream cheese, goat cheese, and Parmesan cheese in a small bowl; stir well. Spread over bread slices.

3 Cut 1 piece of red pepper into 6 julienne strips. Reserve remaining red pepper for another use. Arrange 3 pepper strips over each bread slice; top each slice with a basil sprig.

Yield: 2 appetizer servings (114 calories per serving).

Vegetable-Cheese Linguine

	Vegetable cooking spray
4	ounces fresh shiitake mushrooms, sliced
¼	cup sliced green onions
1	cup torn fresh spinach
1	cup seeded, diced plum tomato
¼	cup minced fresh parsley
2	tablespoons canned low-sodium chicken broth, undiluted
3	ounces linguine, uncooked
3	tablespoons freshly grated Parmesan cheese

1 Coat a large nonstick skillet with cooking spray; place over medium-high heat until hot. Add mushrooms and green onions; sauté 3 minutes. Add spinach and next 3 ingredients; cook 1 minute. Set aside, and keep warm.

2 Cook pasta according to package directions, omitting salt and fat; drain. Place pasta in a large bowl; add cheese, tossing well. Add mushroom mixture, and toss gently. Serve immediately.

Yield: 2 (2-cup) servings (240 calories per serving).

Per Serving:
Carbohydrate 39.3g
Protein 11.9g
Fat 4.4g
Fiber 3.8g
Cholesterol 7mg
Sodium 206mg
Calcium 171mg
Exchanges
2 Vegetable
2 Grain
1 Medium-Fat Meat

Strawberry Sparkler

1	cup sliced fresh strawberries
¼	cup frozen strawberry daiquiri fruit juice concentrate, thawed
¾	cup champagne, chilled
½	cup lemon-flavored sparkling water, chilled
2	fresh strawberries (optional)

1 Place sliced strawberries in container of an electric blender; cover and process until smooth. Pour into a pitcher; add strawberry juice concentrate, and stir well. Cover and chill.

2 Just before serving, stir in champagne and sparkling water. Pour into chilled champagne flutes. Garnish with fresh strawberries, if desired.

Yield: 2 (1-cup) servings (151 calories per serving).

Per Serving:
Carbohydrate 21.0g
Protein 0.7g
Fat 0.3g
Fiber 2.0g
Cholesterol 0mg
Sodium 5mg
Calcium 22mg
Exchanges
1 Fruit
½ Grain

Tropical Dinner
Calypso Beef Tenderloin Steaks

Basil Scalloped Potatoes   Coconut Baby Carrots   Lemon-Sauced Cakes

Serves 6   Total calories per serving: 654

Meal Plan for Tropical Dinner

- Complete step 1 of Calypso Beef Tenderloin Steaks.
- Complete step 1 of Lemon-Sauced Cakes; set aside.
- Make Basil Scalloped Potatoes.
- Make Coconut Baby Carrots; keep warm.
- Complete step 2 of tenderloin steaks.
- Just before serving, complete step 2 of Lemon-Sauced Cakes.

Dinner on the table in 60 minutes

Calypso Beef Tenderloin Steaks

¾ cup canned low-sodium chicken broth, undiluted
½ cup unsweetened orange juice
2½ tablespoons reduced-calorie ketchup
2 tablespoons brown sugar
2 tablespoons lime juice
2 tablespoons dark rum
1 teaspoon ground ginger
¼ teaspoon ground cloves
¼ teaspoon dried thyme
¼ teaspoon ground red pepper
1 large clove garlic, minced
1 (1½-pound) lean boneless beef tenderloin
    Vegetable cooking spray
    Lime slices (optional)
    Fresh basil sprigs (optional)

Per Serving:
Carbohydrate 8.5g
Protein 25.9g
Fat 8.7g
Fiber 0.1g
Cholesterol 75mg
Sodium 71mg
Calcium 16mg
Exchanges
½ Fruit
3½ Lean Meat

1 Combine first 11 ingredients in a bowl; stir well with a wire whisk. Trim fat from tenderloin; cut tenderloin into 6 equal steaks. Place in a large heavy-duty, zip-top plastic bag; pour marinade over steaks. Seal bag; shake well. Marinate in refrigerator 30 minutes, turning bag occasionally.

2 Remove steaks from marinade, reserving marinade. Place steaks on rack of a broiler pan coated with cooking spray. Broil 5½ inches from heat (with electric oven door partially opened) 6 to 8 minutes on each side or to desired degree of doneness, basting frequently with marinade. If desired, garnish with lime slices and basil sprigs.

Yield: 6 servings (233 calories per serving).

Basil Scalloped Potatoes

Per Serving:
Carbohydrate 21.5g
Protein 10.4g
Fat 4.1g
Fiber 2.2g
Cholesterol 14mg
Sodium 232mg
Calcium 300mg
Exchanges
1½ Grain
1 Fat

Vegetable cooking spray
2   cloves garlic, minced
¾   cup skim milk, divided
1   tablespoon all-purpose flour
¾   cup evaporated skimmed milk
2   tablespoons chopped fresh basil
¼   teaspoon salt
¼   teaspoon dried crushed red pepper
⅛   teaspoon ground white pepper
4   cups peeled, thinly sliced baking potato (about 1¾ pounds)
½   cup (2 ounces) shredded Gruyère cheese
2   tablespoons freshly grated Parmesan cheese

1 Coat a large saucepan with cooking spray; place over medium-high heat until hot. Add garlic, and sauté until tender.

2 Combine ¼ cup skim milk and flour; stir with a wire whisk until smooth. Add flour mixture to garlic; cook, stirring constantly, 1 minute or until mixture thickens. Gradually add remaining ½ cup skim milk, evaporated milk, and next 4 ingredients. Bring to a boil, stirring constantly. Add potato.

3 Spoon half of mixture into an 11- x 7- x 1½-inch baking dish coated with cooking spray. Top with half of Gruyère cheese. Repeat layers. Sprinkle with Parmesan cheese. Cover and bake at 350° for 30 minutes. Uncover and bake 15 additional minutes. Let stand 10 minutes before serving.

Yield: 6 (½-cup) servings (161 calories per serving).

"To keep inches off your waist, take inches off your plate. Smaller plates make less food seem like more!" — Jenny

Coconut Baby Carrots

1 (16-ounce) package frozen baby carrots, thawed
2 tablespoons reduce-calorie stick margarine
2 tablespoons honey
2 tablespoons chutney
½ teaspoon mustard seeds
¼ cup unsweetened grated coconut, toasted

1 Combine first 5 ingredients in a large skillet. Cook over medium-high heat until thoroughly heated, stirring occasionally. Transfer to a serving dish; sprinkle with coconut.

Yield: 6 (½-cup) servings (105 calories per serving).

Per Serving:
Carbohydrate 17.7g
Protein 1.1g
Fat 4.2g
Fiber 2.6g
Cholesterol 0mg
Sodium 76mg
Calcium 25mg
Exchanges
2 Vegetable
1 Fat

Lemon-Sauced Cakes

¼ cup sugar
2 teaspoons cornstarch
  Dash of salt
½ cup water
¾ teaspoon grated lemon rind
2½ tablespoons lemon juice
1 tablespoon margarine
8 ounces reduced-fat pound cake
6 tablespoons reduced-calorie whipped topping

1 Combine sugar, cornstarch, and salt in a 2-cup glass measure; add water, and stir until sugar dissolves. Microwave at HIGH for 1 minute; stir well. Microwave at HIGH for 1 to 1½ minutes, stirring at 30-second intervals, until mixture is clear, thickened, and bubbly. Stir in lemon rind, lemon juice, and margarine.

2 Cut pound cake into 6 slices; place on individual serving plates. Top each slice with 2 tablespoons lemon sauce and 1 tablespoon whipped topping.

Yield: 6 servings (155 calories per serving).

Per Serving:
Carbohydrate 30.3g
Protein 1.7g
Fat 3.5g
Fiber 0.5g
Cholesterol 0mg
Sodium 184mg
Calcium 4mg
Exchanges
2 Grain

An Evening in Japan   Egg Drop Soup   Beef Teriyaki

Steamed Rice   Sesame Vegetable Medley   Sweet Oranges with Strawberries

Serves 10   Total calories per serving: 442

Meal Plan for An Evening in Japan

- Complete step 1 of Beef Teriyaki.
- Start step 1 of Sweet Oranges with Strawberries.
- Complete step 2 and start step 3 of teriyaki.
- As beef cooks, prepare Sesame Vegetable Medley.
- Prepare Egg Drop Soup.
- Complete step 4 of teriyaki.
- Complete step 1 of dessert.

Dinner on the table in 50 minutes

~

Egg Drop Soup

2½ quarts water
1   tablespoon chicken-flavored bouillon granules
2   tablespoons low-sodium soy sauce
¼   cup chopped green onion
4   eggs, lightly beaten

1 Combine first 4 ingredients in a large saucepan; bring to boil. Slowly pour eggs into boiling broth. Cook 1 minute. Serve immediately.

Yield: 10 (1-cup) servings (35 calories per serving).

Per Serving:

Carbohydrate 0.7g
Protein 2.7g
Fat 2.3g
Fiber 0.1g
Cholesterol 85mg
Sodium 350mg
Calcium 13mg
Exchange
Free

Beef Teriyaki

Per Serving:
Carbohydrate 3.5g
Protein 22.5g
Fat 6.1g
Fiber 0g
Cholesterol 65mg
Sodium 267mg
Calcium 12mg
Exchanges
3 Lean Meat

¾ cup dry sherry
¾ cup low-sodium soy sauce
1 tablespoon vegetable oil
½ teaspoon dry mustard
⅛ teaspoon onion powder
3 cloves garlic, minced
2 pounds boneless top sirloin steak (1 inch thick)
1½ tablespoons dark corn syrup
1 tablespoon water
2 teaspoons cornstarch
Vegetable cooking spray
1 tablespoon plus 2 teaspoons dry mustard
1 tablespoon water

1 Combine first 6 ingredients, stirring well. Reserve ½ cup mixture. Pour remaining mixture into a large heavy-duty, zip-top plastic bag. Add steak; seal bag, and shake until steak is well coated. Marinate in refrigerator at least 30 minutes but no longer than 4 hours, turning bag occasionally.

2 Combine reserved sherry mixture, corn syrup, 1 tablespoon water, and cornstarch in a small saucepan, stirring well. Bring to a boil over medium-low heat, and cook, stirring constantly, 1 minute. Remove from heat. Set aside, and keep warm.

3 Remove steak from marinade, discarding marinade. Place steak on rack of a broiler pan coated with cooking spray. Broil 5½ inches from heat (with electric oven door partially opened) 6 to 7 minutes on each side or to desired degree of doneness. Slice diagonally across grain into thin slices. Arrange on individual serving plates; brush with cooked sherry mixture.

4 Combine 1 tablespoon plus 2 teaspoons mustard and 1 tablespoon water in a small bowl, stirring well with a wire whisk. Spoon alongside steak strips.

Yield: 10 servings (167 calories per serving).

Sesame Vegetable Medley

1	cup small fresh shiitake mushrooms
	Vegetable cooking spray
2	teaspoons sesame oil
1	pound fresh snow pea pods, trimmed
1	cup diagonally sliced carrot
½	cup canned bamboo shoots, drained
1	clove garlic, minced
2	tablespoons water
1	tablespoon low-sodium soy sauce
2	teaspoons sugar
¼	teaspoon cornstarch
¼	teaspoon chicken-flavored bouillon granules
¼	teaspoon Dijon mustard
1	tablespoon sesame seeds, toasted

Per Serving:
Carbohydrate 10.0g
Protein 2.2g
Fat 1.6g
Fiber 2.2g
Cholesterol 0mg
Sodium 70mg
Calcium 25mg
Exchanges
2 Vegetable

1 Remove and discard mushroom stems. Coat a large nonstick skillet with cooking spray; add oil. Place over medium-high heat until hot. Add mushroom caps, snow peas, and next 3 ingredients; sauté 2 minutes.

2 Combine water and next 5 ingredients; add to vegetable mixture. Cook, stirring constantly, until slightly thickened. Sprinkle with sesame seeds.

Yield: 10 (½-cup) servings (64 calories per serving).

Sweet Oranges with Strawberries

¾	cup water
¾	cup rosé wine
½	cup sugar
2	whole cloves
2	(1-inch) slices peeled gingerroot
1	(2-inch) stick cinnamon
½	vanilla bean, split lengthwise
6	small oranges, peeled and cut crosswise into ⅛-inch slices
2	cups halved fresh strawberries

Per Serving:
Carbohydrate 17.2g
Protein 0.6g
Fat 0.2g
Fiber 2.6g
Cholesterol 0mg
Sodium 2mg
Calcium 22mg
Exchange
1 Fruit

1 Bring first 7 ingredients to a boil in a saucepan; cover, reduce heat, and simmer 15 minutes. Pour through a strainer into a bowl; discard solids in strainer. Add orange slices to hot syrup. Chill. To serve, stir in strawberries.

Yield: 10 (½-cup) servings (68 calories per serving).

Recipes

Get Ready To Enjoy

Think about what you'd like to eat, and anticipate the pleasure. Think about sharing a meal, and what it means to your family. Whether you're having a backyard picnic, a neighborhood gathering, a weeknight dinner, or a last-minute lunch, you'll find ideas in the following recipe chapters to help you create exciting meals. And rest assured that they taste great and are quick and easy to prepare. That's because each was developed and taste-tested to combine exceptional flavor with low-fat cooking techniques and the latest principles of good nutrition.

But where do you begin? By making gradual changes in eating habits, increasing physical activity, and taking a little time for relaxation, you'll have more energy and a greater sense of well-being. You'll also improve your chances of living longer and avoiding some of the major diseases of our time. But most importantly, you'll improve your quality of life, beginning now.

If you make healthy eating part of your lifestyle, there will rarely be an occasion when you'll feel you can't eat as healthfully as you'd like.

•*Entertaining a few special friends?* Start off with Garbanzo Guacamole (page 70) and Mock Margaritas (page 79).

•*For an impressive entrée,* serve Holiday Turkey Cutlets (page 149) or Grilled Herbed Salmon (page 156).

•*To round out a meal,* the rich-tasting but low-fat goodness of Peach Trifle (page 100) or Chocolate-Cherry Squares (page 111) will be irresistible to young and old alike.

•*In the mood for something spicy?* Try Cuban Black Bean Soup (page 202). Something Oriental in mind? How about Thai Chicken Barbecue (page 145)?

Get your family involved in choosing recipes and planning menus too. By showing them that nutritious can be delicious, you'll be encouraging a healthy pattern of eating for the entire family.

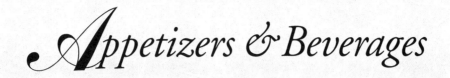

Appetizers & Beverages

Garbanzo Guacamole (page 70), Mock Margaritas (page 79)

Garbanzo Guacamole

Time: Prep 15 minutes; Chill 30 minutes

Per Tablespoon:
Carbohydrate 1.9g
Protein 0.5g
Fat 0.5g
Fiber 0.4g
Cholesterol 0mg
Sodium 20mg
Calcium 5mg
Exchange
Free

⅔ cup canned garbanzo beans, drained
1 tablespoon lemon juice
1 large clove garlic, halved
¾ cup coarsely chopped onion
½ cup peeled, cubed avocado
2 tablespoons canned chopped green chiles
¼ teaspoon salt
¼ teaspoon pepper
1 cup seeded, finely chopped tomato
½ cup finely chopped green onions

1 Position knife blade in food processor bowl; add first 3 ingredients. Process 20 seconds, scraping sides of processor bowl once. Add ¾ cup chopped onion and next 4 ingredients; pulse 5 times or until mixture is chunky.

2 Transfer mixture to a medium bowl; stir in tomato and green onions. Cover and chill thoroughly. Serve with commercial baked tortilla chips.

Yield: 2 cups (13 calories per tablespoon).

Fat Facts About Avocados

Most fruits and vegetables are virtually fat-free—except avocados. A medium avocado contains about 300 calories, with a whopping 88% of those calories from fat. Although this fat is monounsaturated (the kind that may help lower blood cholesterol levels), you can't ignore the fact that avocados are mostly fat.

But you don't have to eliminate this fruit from your diet. Instead, use avocados in reduced amounts by combining them with other ingredients—like we've done in Garbanzo Guacamole. You'll still enjoy the flavor but without all that fat.

Nacho Olive Dip

Time: Prep 5 minutes; Chill at least 2 hours

1	cup nonfat sour cream	
½	cup nonfat mayonnaise	
1	(4½-ounce) can chopped ripe olives, drained	
¾	cup minced green onions	
¾	cup seeded, chopped tomato	
⅔	cup minced fresh cilantro	
2	tablespoons fresh lime juice	
2	cloves garlic, minced	
1	teaspoon hot sauce	

Per Tablespoon:
Carbohydrate 1.3g
Protein 0.4g
Fat 0.3g
Fiber 0.2g
Cholesterol 0mg
Sodium 55mg
Calcium 9mg
Exchange
Free

1 Combine all ingredients in a medium bowl. Cover and chill at least 2 hours. Serve with raw vegetables, baked tortilla chips, pita wedges, commercial breadsticks, or melba rounds.

Yield: 3¼ cups (9 calories per tablespoon).

Party Spinach Dip

Time: Prep 10 minutes; Chill at least 3 hours

1	(12-ounce) carton 1% low-fat cottage cheese	
1	(10-ounce) package frozen chopped spinach, thawed	
1	(8-ounce) can water chestnuts, drained and chopped	
½	cup low-fat sour cream	
¼	cup dry vegetable soup mix	
2	teaspoons grated onion	
1	teaspoon lemon juice	

Per Tablespoon:
Carbohydrate 0.9g
Protein 0.9g
Fat 0.3g
Fiber 0.2g
Cholesterol 1mg
Sodium 26mg
Calcium 11mg
Exchange
Free

1 Position knife blade in food processor bowl; add cottage cheese. Process until smooth, scraping sides of processor bowl once. Transfer to a bowl.

2 Drain spinach; press between paper towels until barely moist.

3 Add spinach, water chestnuts, and remaining ingredients to cottage cheese; stir well. Cover and chill at least 3 hours. Serve with melba rounds or raw vegetables.

Yield: 4 cups (9 calories per tablespoon).

Three-Cheese Spread

Time: Prep 5 minutes; Chill at least 8 hours

Per Tablespoon:
Carbohydrate 0.8g
Protein 2.7g
Fat 1.0g
Fiber 0.1g
Cholesterol 5mg
Sodium 93mg
Calcium 64mg
Exchange
Free

1   (8-ounce) package nonfat cream cheese, softened
1   cup (4 ounces) shredded nonfat Cheddar cheese
½   cup crumbled blue cheese
¼   cup chopped almonds, toasted
2   tablespoons skim milk
1   teaspoon low-sodium Worcestershire sauce

1 Combine all ingredients in a small bowl, stirring until smooth. Cover and chill 8 hours.

2 Let cheese mixture stand at room temperature 30 minutes before serving. Serve with fat-free crackers, apple wedges, or pear wedges.

Yield: 2 cups (24 calories per tablespoon).

Quick Fruit Dip

Time: Prep 5 minutes

Per Tablespoon:
Carbohydrate 2.1g
Protein 0.7g
Fat 0.2g
Fiber 0g
Cholesterol 1mg
Sodium 10mg
Calcium 26mg
Exchange
Free

1⅓ cups vanilla low-fat yogurt
¼   cup low-sugar orange marmalade
¼   teaspoon ground cinnamon

1 Combine all ingredients; cover and chill. Serve with fresh fruit.

Yield: 1½ cups (13 calories per tablespoon).

Healthy Partners for Dips and Spreads

Try these low-fat accompaniments:

For Savory Dips and Spreads: Fresh vegetables like broccoli and cauliflower flowerets, carrot and celery sticks, squash slices, Sugar Snap peas, and cherry tomatoes. Or try fat-free crackers or no-oil baked tortilla chips.

For Sweet Dips: Fresh fruit such as apple and pear wedges, grapes, strawberries, pineapple chunks, peach slices, and melon cubes. Or use cubed fat-free pound cake or angel food cake, and fat-free cookies.

Orange-Poppy Seed Dip

Orange-Poppy Seed Dip

Time: Prep 10 minutes; Chill at least 25 minutes

½   cup vanilla low-fat yogurt
¼   cup light process cream cheese product, softened
¼   cup orange marmalade
1   teaspoon poppy seeds
    Orange curls (optional)

Per Tablespoon:
Carbohydrate 6.1g
Protein 1.0g
Fat 1.0g
Fiber 0g
Cholesterol 3mg
Sodium 36mg
Calcium 29mg
Exchange
Free

1 Spoon yogurt onto several layers of heavy-duty paper towels, and spread to ½-inch thickness. Cover with additional paper towels; let stand 5 minutes. Scrape yogurt into a medium bowl, using a rubber spatula.

2 Add cream cheese to yogurt. Beat at medium speed of an electric mixer until smooth. Stir in marmalade and poppy seeds. Cover and chill at least 25 minutes.

3 Stir before serving. Garnish with orange curls, if desired. Serve with assorted fresh fruit. Store remaining dip, tightly covered, in the refrigerator up to 5 days.

Yield: ¾ cup (36 calories per tablespoon).

Southwestern New Potatoes

Time: Prep 30 minutes; Cook 10 minutes

Per Appetizer:
Carbohydrate 7.9g
Protein 1.6g
Fat 0.1g
Fiber 0.8g
Cholesterol 0mg
Sodium 58mg
Calcium 8mg
Exchange
½ Grain

15	small round red potatoes (about 1½ pounds)
½	cup nonfat sour cream
2	tablespoons canned chopped green chiles
1	tablespoon diced pimiento
1	teaspoon ground cumin
¼	teaspoon salt
⅛	teaspoon ground red pepper

1 Arrange potatoes in a vegetable steamer over boiling water. Cover and steam 15 to 20 minutes or until tender. Remove from steamer; let cool.

2 Scoop out centers of potatoes with a melon-ball scoop or small spoon; set aside potato shells.

3 Mash potato pulp at medium speed of an electric mixer until smooth. Stir in sour cream and remaining ingredients. Spoon or pipe evenly into potato shells, using a decorating bag fitted with a large round tip.

4 Place stuffed potatoes on a baking sheet. Bake at 425° for 10 to 15 minutes or until thoroughly heated.

Yield: 15 appetizers (39 calories each).

Lemon-Dijon Marinated Shrimp

Time: Prep 45 minutes; Marinate 4 hours

1	quart water
36	unpeeled medium-size fresh shrimp (about 1½ pounds)
1	cup water
⅓	cup lemon juice
2	tablespoons Dijon mustard
2	cloves garlic, minced
¾	teaspoon dried dillweed
½	teaspoon peeled, minced gingerroot
¼	teaspoon crushed red pepper
36	fresh snow pea pods, trimmed

Per Appetizer:
Carbohydrate 0.6g
Protein 2.1g
Fat 0.2g
Fiber 0.1g
Cholesterol 18mg
Sodium 46mg
Calcium 6mg
Exchange
Free

1 Bring 1 quart water to a boil in a Dutch oven; add shrimp, and cook 3 to 5 minutes or until shrimp are done. Drain shrimp well; rinse with cold water. Peel and devein shrimp, and place in a shallow baking dish.

2 Combine 1 cup water and next 6 ingredients in a small bowl; stir well. Pour over shrimp; toss gently. Cover and marinate in refrigerator 4 to 6 hours, stirring occasionally.

3 Arrange snow peas in a vegetable steamer over boiling water. Cover and steam 3 to 5 minutes or until crisp-tender. Remove snow peas from steamer, and chill.

4 Wrap a snow pea around each shrimp; secure with a wooden pick, and arrange on a serving platter.

Yield: 3 dozen appetizers (13 calories each).

Timesaver for Shrimp

Serving shrimp at your next party? Save yourself time in the kitchen by purchasing peeled and deveined shrimp and having them steamed at the supermarket. Two pounds of unpeeled fresh shrimp equal 1 pound of cooked, peeled, and deveined shrimp.

Cranberry Chicken Salad Cups

Cranberry Chicken Salad Cups

Time: Prep 20 minutes; Cook 8 minutes

Per Appetizer:
Carbohydrate 5.8g
Protein 3.3g
Fat 0.5g
Fiber 0g
Cholesterol 8mg
Sodium 72mg
Calcium 7mg
Exchange
½ Grain

1½ cups diced cooked chicken breast (skinned before cooking and cooked without salt)
½ cup canned mandarin oranges in water, drained
¼ cup nonfat mayonnaise
2 tablespoons minced green pepper
3 tablespoons jellied whole-berry cranberry sauce
1 teaspoon minced crystallized ginger
2 teaspoons honey
½ teaspoon prepared horseradish
32 fresh or frozen wonton skins, thawed
Vegetable cooking spray
Fresh parsley sprigs (optional)
Fresh cranberries (optional)

1 Combine first 8 ingredients in a small bowl; stir well. Cover and chill.

2 Place 1 wonton skin in each of 32 miniature (1¾-inch) muffin cups coated with cooking spray. Press wontons against bottoms and up sides of cups. Coat wontons with cooking spray. Bake at 350° for 8 minutes or until wontons are crisp and golden. Let cool completely in pans.

3 Spoon chicken mixture evenly into wonton cups. Remove wonton cups from pans, and serve immediately. If desired, garnish with parsley sprigs and cranberries.

Yield: 32 appetizers (42 calories each).

Tuna and Sun-Dried Tomato Crostini

Time: Prep 10 minutes; Cook 15 minutes

18	(⅓-inch-thick) slices French baguette
	Olive oil-flavored vegetable cooking spray
3	tablespoons minced fresh basil
2	tablespoons nonfat mayonnaise
2	tablespoons plain nonfat yogurt
1	teaspoon crushed garlic
1	(6⅛-ounce) can 60% less-salt tuna in water, drained
⅓	cup minced green onions
2	tablespoons minced sun-dried tomato
1	tablespoon chopped ripe olives
18	large arugula or Bibb lettuce leaves

Per Serving:
Carbohydrate 11.7g
Protein 8.4g
Fat 1.2g
Fiber 0.6g
Cholesterol 9mg
Sodium 252mg
Calcium 36mg
Exchanges
1 Grain
1 Meat

1 Spray both sides of each bread slice with cooking spray; arrange in a single layer on a baking sheet. Bake at 300° for 15 minutes or until lightly browned.

2 Combine basil, mayonnaise, yogurt, and garlic; stir well. Add tuna and next 3 ingredients; stir well.

3 To serve, place 1 arugula leaf on each bread slice; top each with 1 table-spoon tuna mixture.

Yield: 6 appetizer servings (90 calories per serving).

Antipasto Kabobs

Antipasto Kabobs

Time: Prep 15 minutes; Marinate 30 minutes

Per Kabob:		
Carbohydrate 4.6g	1	medium carrot, scraped
Protein 5.8g	1	medium-size yellow squash, cut into ¼-inch slices
Fat 3.3g	1	small green pepper, seeded and cut into 1-inch pieces
Fiber 1.3g	8	cherry tomatoes
Cholesterol 5mg	8	ripe olives
Sodium 58mg	8	small fresh mushrooms
Calcium 129mg	¼	cup white wine vinegar
Exchanges	¼	cup water
1 Vegetable	1	tablespoon olive oil
½ Medium-Fat Meat	1	teaspoon dried Italian seasoning
	⅛	teaspoon garlic powder
	⅛	teaspoon pepper
	4	ounces reduced-fat Monterey Jack cheese, cubed

78

1 Slice carrot with a vegetable peeler lengthwise into long thin strips. Place strips in a large shallow dish. Add squash and next 4 ingredients.

2 Combine vinegar and next 5 ingredients in a jar; cover tightly, and shake vigorously. Pour over vegetables. Cover; marinate in refrigerator 30 minutes.

3 Thread vegetables and cheese alternately onto 8 (6-inch) wooden skewers.

Yield: 8 kabobs (68 calories each).

Mock Margaritas

Time: Prep 5 minutes; Freeze 30 minutes

1	**(6-ounce) can frozen lemonade concentrate, thawed and undiluted**
1	**(6-ounce) can frozen limeade concentrate, thawed and undiluted**
½	**cup sifted powdered sugar**
3¼	**cups crushed ice**
1½	**cups club soda, chilled**
	Lime slices (optional)

Per Serving:
Carbohydrate 37.3g
Protein 0.1g
Fat 0.1g
Fiber 0.1g
Cholesterol 0mg
Sodium 13mg
Calcium 6mg
Exchanges
2 Fruit

1 Combine first 4 ingredients in a large plastic container, stirring until sugar dissolves. Freeze mixture. Remove mixture from freezer 30 minutes before serving.

2 Spoon mixture into container of an electric blender; add club soda. Cover and process until smooth. Pour into glasses; garnish with lime slices, if desired.

Yield: 6 (1-cup) servings (143 calories per serving).

"I like to drink a big glass of water before cocktail parties where hors d'oeuvres are served. Sometimes I drink two. That way my hunger is quelled and I'm not tempted to overindulge."— Jenny

Citrus-Mint Cooler

Time: Prep 5 minutes; Chill at least 8 hours

Per Serving:
Carbohydrate 34.3g
Protein 1.0g
Fat 0.2g
Fiber 0.1g
Cholesterol 0mg
Sodium 14mg
Calcium 14mg
Exchanges
2 Fruit

1   cup loosely packed fresh mint leaves
2   cups unsweetened pink grapefruit juice
1   cup unsweetened orange juice
⅓   cup sugar
1   cup lemon-flavored sparkling water, chilled
     Fresh mint sprigs (optional)

1 Combine first 4 ingredients in a medium bowl, stirring well. Cover and chill at least 8 hours, stirring occasionally.

2 Pour mixture through a wire-mesh strainer into a pitcher, discarding mint. Just before serving, stir in sparkling water. Garnish with mint sprigs, if desired.

Yield: 4 (1-cup) servings (139 calories per serving).

Melon Lime Cooler

Time: Prep 5 minutes; Freeze 30 minutes

Per Serving:
Carbohydrate 32.4g
Protein 1.5g
Fat 0.7g
Fiber 1.8g
Cholesterol 0mg
Sodium 59mg
Calcium 35mg
Exchanges
1 Fruit
1 Grain

4½ cups cubed honeydew melon (about 1 small)
1½ cups lime sherbet
2   tablespoons lime juice
     Fresh strawberries (optional)

1 Place melon cubes in a single layer on a baking sheet. Cover and freeze 30 minutes or until firm.

2 Position knife blade in food processor bowl; add frozen melon, sherbet, and lime juice. Process until smooth. Pour into glasses. Garnish with strawberries, if desired. Serve immediately.

Yield: 5 (1-cup) servings (131 calories per serving).

Melon Lime Cooler, Citrus-Mint Cooler

Chocolate-Pecan Coffee

Time: Prep 5 minutes

½   cup medium-grind pecan-flavored coffee
1   tablespoon unsweetened cocoa
½   teaspoon ground cinnamon
5   cups water
3   tablespoons chocolate-flavored syrup

Per Serving:
Carbohydrate 6.8g
Protein 0.7g
Fat 0.3g
Fiber 0g
Cholesterol 0mg
Sodium 10mg
Calcium 9mg
Exchange
½ Grain

1 Combine first 3 ingredients in basket of a drip coffee maker or electric percolator. Place water in pot. Prepare coffee according to manufacturer's instructions.

2 Stir in chocolate syrup.

Yield: 6 (¾-cup) servings (32 calories per serving).

Frosted Cappuccino

Time: Prep 5 minutes

Per Serving:
Carbohydrate 22.7g
Protein 2.1g
Fat 0.0g
Fiber 0g
Cholesterol 0mg
Sodium 47mg
Calcium 82mg
Exchanges
1½ Grain

2 cups brewed espresso coffee, chilled
2 cups vanilla nonfat ice cream
½ teaspoon vanilla extract
Ground cinnamon (optional)

1 Combine first 3 ingredients in container of an electric blender; cover and process until smooth. Pour into glasses. Sprinkle each serving with cinnamon, if desired. Serve immediately.

Yield: 4 (1-cup) servings (104 calories per serving).

Vanilla Cream Alexander

Time: Prep 5 minutes

Per Serving:
Carbohydrate 12.7g
Protein 3.8g
Fat 0.2g
Fiber 0g
Cholesterol 2mg
Sodium 63mg
Calcium 141mg
Exchanges
½ Grain
½ Milk

2¾ cups skim milk
1 cup vanilla nonfat ice cream
2 tablespoons brandy
2 tablespoons crème de cacao
Ground nutmeg (optional)

1 Combine first 4 ingredients in container of an electric blender; cover and process until smooth. Pour into glasses. Sprinkle with nutmeg, if desired. Serve immediately.

Yield: 7 (¾-cup) servings (88 calories per serving).

Breads

Parmesan Breadsticks and Cinnamon Breadsticks (page 88),
Orange-Glazed Breadsticks (page 89)

Fresh Chive Buttermilk Biscuits

Time: Prep 15 minutes; Cook 10 minutes

Per Biscuit:
Carbohydrate 9.4g
Protein 1.6g
Fat 1.8g
Fiber 0.3g
Cholesterol 0mg
Sodium 110mg
Calcium 43mg
Exchange
1 Grain

2   cups all-purpose flour
1   tablespoon baking powder
¼   teaspoon baking soda
¼   teaspoon salt
½   teaspoon sugar
3   tablespoons chopped fresh chives
3   tablespoons margarine
¾   cup plus 1 tablespoon nonfat buttermilk
1   tablespoon all-purpose flour
¼   teaspoon paprika

1 Combine first 6 ingredients in a medium bowl; cut in margarine with a pastry blender until mixture resembles coarse meal. Add buttermilk, stirring just until dry ingredients are moistened.

2 Sprinkle 1 tablespoon flour evenly over work surface. Turn dough out onto floured surface, and knead 10 to 12 times. Roll dough to ½-inch thickness; cut with a 2-inch biscuit cutter.

3 Place on an ungreased baking sheet, and sprinkle with paprika. Bake at 425° for 10 to 12 minutes or until biscuits are golden.

Yield: 21 biscuits (60 calories each).

"Looks can be deceiving. A croissant, for example, may seem light and airy, but it contains 15 grams more fat and 200 more calories than a Fresh Chive Buttermilk Biscuit. For the lowdown on fat and calories, be sure to read nutritional labels." —Jenny

Whole Wheat Yeast Biscuits

Time: Prep 15 minutes; Cook 10 minutes

1	package active dry yeast
⅓	cup warm water (105° to 115°)
2½	cups whole wheat flour
½	cup all-purpose flour
2	teaspoons baking powder
½	teaspoon baking soda
½	teaspoon salt
½	teaspoon dried oregano
½	teaspoon dried basil
1	tablespoon sugar
3	tablespoons margarine
1	cup nonfat buttermilk
2	tablespoons all-purpose flour
	Vegetable cooking spray

Per Biscuit:

Carbohydrate 12.6g
Protein 2.5g
Fat 1.8g
Fiber 1.8g
Cholesterol 0mg
Sodium 119mg
Calcium 41mg
Exchange
1 Grain

1 Combine yeast and warm water in a small bowl; let stand 5 minutes.

2 Combine whole wheat flour and next 7 ingredients in a large bowl; cut in margarine with a pastry blender until flour mixture resembles coarse meal. Add yeast mixture and buttermilk to flour mixture, stirring just until dry ingredients are moistened.

3 Sprinkle 2 tablespoons flour evenly over work surface. Turn dough out onto floured surface, and knead 3 or 4 times. Roll dough to ½-inch thickness; cut with a 2-inch biscuit cutter. Place on baking sheets coated with cooking spray. Bake at 400° for 10 to 12 minutes or until biscuits are lightly browned.

Yield: 2 dozen biscuits (73 calories each).

Fruited Scones

Fruited Scones

Time: Prep 15 minutes; Cook 15 minutes

Per Scone:		
Carbohydrate 28.4g	2	cups all-purpose flour
Protein 3.6g	1	tablespoon baking powder
Fat 3.8g	¼	teaspoon baking soda
Fiber 0.9g	¼	teaspoon salt
Cholesterol 1mg	1	tablespoon sugar
Sodium 153mg	½	teaspoon grated orange rind
Calcium 114mg	3	tablespoons margarine
Exchanges	½	cup diced dried mixed fruit
½ Fruit	¾	cup nonfat buttermilk
1½ Grain	1	tablespoon all-purpose flour
1 Fat	1	tablespoon skim milk
		Vegetable cooking spray
	2	teaspoons sugar

1 Combine first 6 ingredients in a medium bowl; cut in margarine with a pastry blender until mixture resembles coarse meal. Stir in dried fruit. Add buttermilk, stirring with a fork just until dry ingredients are moistened.

2 Sprinkle 1 tablespoon flour evenly over work surface. Turn dough out onto floured surface, and knead 10 to 12 times. Roll dough into an 8-inch circle, and cut into 10 wedges. Brush evenly with skim milk.

3 Transfer wedges to a baking sheet coated with cooking spray. Sprinkle evenly with 2 teaspoons sugar. Bake at 425° for 15 minutes or until golden. Serve warm.

Yield: 10 scones (161 calories each).

Easy Mustard Breadsticks

Time: Prep 15 minutes; Cook 12 minutes

1   (11-ounce) package refrigerated cracked wheat and honey twists
1   tablespoon reduced-calorie margarine
1   tablespoon coarse-grained mustard
1   tablespoon beer
1   tablespoon plus 2 teaspoons grated Parmesan cheese

Per Breadstick:
Carbohydrate 14.2g
Protein 2.3g
Fat 3.0g
Fiber 1.0g
Cholesterol 0mg
Sodium 181mg
Calcium 9mg
Exchanges
1 Grain
1 Fat

1 Unroll and twist dough according to package directions. Place twists on an ungreased baking sheet.

2 Combine margarine, mustard, and beer in a small saucepan; cook over low heat, stirring frequently, until margarine melts and mixture is smooth. Brush mustard mixture over twists; sprinkle each with ½ teaspoon Parmesan cheese.

3 Bake at 375° for 12 to 13 minutes or until golden.

Yield: 10 breadsticks (90 calories each).

Parmesan Breadsticks

Time: Prep 20 minutes; Rise 20 minutes; Cook 12 minutes

Per Breadstick:
Carbohydrate 10.6g
Protein 2.0g
Fat 1.2g
Fiber 0g
Cholesterol 1mg
Sodium 121mg
Calcium 26mg
Exchange
1 Grain

1	(16-ounce) package hot roll mix
¼	cup grated Parmesan cheese
1	cup very warm water (120° to 130°)
1	egg white, lightly beaten
2	tablespoons vegetable oil
1	teaspoon dried Italian seasoning
	Butter-flavored vegetable cooking spray
2	tablespoons plus 2 teaspoons grated Parmesan cheese

1 Combine roll mix, yeast from packet, and ¼ cup cheese in a bowl. Add water and next 3 ingredients; stir until moistened. Shape into a ball. Turn out onto a lightly floured surface; knead until smooth and elastic (about 5 minutes). Cover; let rest 5 minutes.

2 Roll dough into a 16- x 12-inch rectangle on a lightly floured surface. Cut rectangle crosswise with a pastry cutter to form 16 strips. Cut strips in half crosswise to form 32 (6-inch) strips.

3 Twist each strip 5 or 6 times; place on baking sheets coated with cooking spray. Spray tops of strips with cooking spray; sprinkle each strip with ¼ teaspoon cheese.

4 Cover; let rise in a warm place (85°), free from drafts, 20 to 30 minutes or until doubled in bulk. Bake at 375° for 12 minutes or until golden.

Yield: 32 breadsticks (63 calories each).

Cinnamon Breadsticks

Per Breadstick:
Carbohydrate 11.7g
Protein 1.6g
Fat 1.8g
Fiber 0g
Cholesterol 0mg
Sodium 115mg
Calcium 11mg
Exchange
1 Grain

Follow directions for steps 1 through 3, omitting cheese and Italian seasoning. Combine ¼ cup sugar and ¾ teaspoon ground cinnamon. Brush strips with ¼ cup reduced-calorie stick margarine, melted; sprinkle with cinnamon mixture. Let rise, and bake as directed in step 4.

Yield: 32 breadsticks (71 calories each).

Orange-Glazed Breadsticks

Follow directions for steps 1 through 3, omitting cheese and Italian seasoning and adding 1 tablespoon grated orange rind. Let rise, and bake as directed in step 4. Combine 1¼ cups sifted powdered sugar, 1½ tablespoons skim milk, and ¼ teaspoon orange extract. Drizzle over breadsticks.

Yield: 32 breadsticks (77 calories each).

Per Breadstick:

Carbohydrate 15.2g
Protein 1.6g
Fat 0.9g
Fiber 0g
Cholesterol 0mg
Sodium 102mg
Calcium 12mg
Exchange
1 Grain

Blueberry Bran Muffins

Time: Prep 10 minutes; Cook 18 minutes

1½ cups all-purpose flour
½ cup unprocessed wheat bran
2 teaspoons baking powder
¼ teaspoon salt
¾ cup sugar
¾ cup skim milk
2 tablespoons vegetable oil
1 egg, lightly beaten
1 teaspoon vanilla extract
1½ cups fresh or frozen blueberries, thawed
Vegetable cooking spray

Per Muffin:

Carbohydrate 22.4g
Protein 2.4g
Fat 2.5g
Fiber 1.8g
Cholesterol 14mg
Sodium 48mg
Calcium 54mg
Exchanges
½ Fruit
1 Grain
1 Fat

1 Combine first 5 ingredients in a medium bowl; make a well in center of mixture.

2 Combine milk and next 3 ingredients; add to dry ingredients, stirring just until dry ingredients are moistened. Fold in blueberries.

3 Spoon batter into muffin pans coated with cooking spray, filling two-thirds full. Bake at 400° for 18 to 20 minutes or until golden. Remove from pans immediately.

Yield: 16 muffins (118 calories each).

Carrot and Pineapple Muffins

Time: Prep 15 minutes; Cook 20 minutes

Per Muffin:
Carbohydrate 19.4g
Protein 2.2g
Fat 4.7g
Fiber 0.7g
Cholesterol 15mg
Sodium 110mg
Calcium 28mg
Exchanges
1 Grain
1 Fat

1¾	cups all-purpose flour
1	teaspoon baking soda
¼	teaspoon salt
1	teaspoon ground cinnamon
¼	teaspoon ground allspice
⅓	cup sugar
1	(8-ounce) can crushed pineapple in juice, undrained
1	cup shredded carrot
¼	cup vegetable oil
3	tablespoons skim milk
1	egg, lightly beaten
	Vegetable cooking spray

1 Combine first 6 ingredients in a medium bowl; make a well in center of mixture.

2 Combine pineapple, carrot, oil, milk, and egg; add to dry ingredients, stirring just until dry ingredients are moistened.

3 Spoon batter into muffin pans coated with cooking spray, filling two-thirds full. Bake at 400° for 20 to 25 minutes or until golden. Remove from pans immediately.

Yield: 14 muffins (127 calories each).

Did You Know?
To reheat leftover muffins, wrap them loosely in aluminum foil and heat at 350° for 8 to 10 minutes. Or wrap in a paper towel or napkin and microwave at HIGH for 15 to 30 seconds per muffin or until warm to the touch.

Zucchini Corn Muffins

Time: Prep 15 minutes; Cook 20 minutes

¾	cup all-purpose flour
¼	cup yellow cornmeal
¾	teaspoon baking powder
¼	teaspoon baking soda
⅛	teaspoon salt
⅛	teaspoon ground cumin
1	cup shredded zucchini
2	tablespoons vegetable oil
2	tablespoons honey
1	egg white, lightly beaten
1	teaspoon skim milk
	Vegetable cooking spray

Per Muffin:
Carbohydrate 23.1g
Protein 3.0g
Fat 5.1g
Fiber 0.8g
Cholesterol 0mg
Sodium 129mg
Calcium 39mg
Exchanges
1½ Grain
1 Fat

1 Combine first 6 ingredients; stir. Add zucchini to flour mixture; make a well in center of mixture.

2 Combine oil, honey, egg white, and milk; add to dry ingredients, stirring just until dry ingredients are moistened.

3 Spoon batter into muffin pans coated with cooking spray, filling two-thirds full. Bake at 375° for 20 minutes or until golden.

Yield: 6 muffins (148 calories each).

Gingerbread Pancakes

Gingerbread Pancakes

Time: Prep 15 minutes; Cook 12 minutes

Per Pancake:
Carbohydrate 18.0g
Protein 4.0g
Fat 3.0g
Fiber 1.8g
Cholesterol 32mg
Sodium 150mg
Calcium 70mg
Exchanges
1 Grain
1 Fat

2	teaspoons instant coffee granules
¼	cup boiling water
¾	cup whole wheat flour
¼	cup all-purpose flour
1	teaspoon baking powder
¼	teaspoon salt
½	teaspoon ground ginger
¼	teaspoon ground cinnamon
⅛	teaspoon ground cloves
3	tablespoons brown sugar
⅔	cup skim milk
1	egg, lightly beaten
1	tablespoon vegetable oil
	Apple butter (optional)

1 Combine coffee granules and boiling water, stirring until granules dissolve. Cool completely.

2 Combine whole wheat flour and next 7 ingredients in a medium bowl; make a well in center of mixture.

3 Combine coffee mixture, milk, egg, and oil; add mixture to dry ingredients, stirring just until dry ingredients are moistened.

4 Preheat nonstick griddle to 325°. For each pancake, pour ¼ cup batter onto hot griddle; spread batter to a 5-inch circle. Cook pancakes until tops are covered with bubbles and edges look cooked; turn pancakes, and cook other side. Serve with apple butter, if desired.

Yield: 7 (5-inch) pancakes (113 calories each).

Whole Wheat Buttermilk Pancakes

Time: Prep 15 minutes; Cook 12 minutes

1½ cups all-purpose flour
½   cup whole wheat flour
1   teaspoon baking soda
¼   teaspoon salt
2   teaspoons sugar
2   cups nonfat buttermilk
2   eggs, lightly beaten
     Vegetable cooking spray

Per Pancake:
Carbohydrate 11.6g
Protein 3.1g
Fat 0.9g
Fiber 0.7g
Cholesterol 24mg
Sodium 114mg
Calcium 47mg
Exchange
1 Grain

1 Combine first 5 ingredients in a large bowl; make a well in center of mixture.

2 Combine buttermilk and eggs; add to dry ingredients, stirring just until dry ingredients are moistened.

3 For each pancake, pour ¼ cup batter onto a hot griddle or skillet coated with cooking spray. Cook pancakes until tops are covered with bubbles and edges look cooked. Turn pancakes, and cook other side.

Yield: 18 (4-inch) pancakes (67 calories each).

Apple-Yogurt Bread

Time: Prep 15 minutes; Cook 40 minutes

Per Slice:
Carbohydrate 17.4g
Protein 3.0g
Fat 3.8g
Fiber 1.1g
Cholesterol 1mg
Sodium 137mg
Calcium 58mg
Exchanges
1 Grain
1 Fat

1	cup whole wheat flour
¾	cup all-purpose flour
1½	teaspoons baking powder
1	teaspoon baking soda
¼	teaspoon salt
½	teaspoon ground cinnamon
⅓	cup firmly packed brown sugar
1	(8-ounce) carton Dutch apple low-fat yogurt with fruit on the bottom
½	cup frozen egg substitute, thawed
¼	cup vegetable oil
2	tablespoons skim milk
	Vegetable cooking spray

1 Combine first 7 ingredients in a large bowl; stir well.

2 Combine yogurt, egg substitute, oil, and milk; add to flour mixture, stirring just until dry ingredients are moistened.

3 Spoon batter into an 8½- x 4½- x 3-inch loafpan coated with cooking spray. Bake at 350° for 40 minutes or until a wooden pick inserted in center comes out clean. Cool in pan 10 minutes; remove from pan, and let cool completely on a wire rack.

Yield: 16 (½-inch) slices (113 calories per slice).

"While the loaves are still warm and the aroma of freshly baked bread fills my kitchen, it's hard to resist eating a slice or two right away. Butter or margarine is tempting, but a low-fat preserve tastes just as good." — Jenny

Cinnamon-Raisin Batter Bread

Time: Prep 15 minutes; Rise 40 minutes; Cook 35 minutes

3	cups all-purpose flour, divided
2	tablespoons sugar
1	teaspoon ground cinnamon
¼	teaspoon salt
¼	teaspoon ground allspice
1	package active dry yeast
1	cup skim milk
¼	cup molasses
2	tablespoons margarine
1	egg, lightly beaten
½	cup raisins
	Vegetable cooking spray

Per Slice:

Carbohydrate 24.4g

Protein 3.1g

Fat 1.8g

Fiber 1.0g

Cholesterol 12mg

Sodium 60mg

Calcium 34mg

Exchanges

1½ Grain

1 Combine 1½ cups flour, sugar, and next 4 ingredients in a large bowl; stir well. Set flour mixture aside.

2 Combine milk, molasses, and margarine in a small saucepan; cook over medium heat until very warm (120° to 130°). Gradually add to flour mixture, beating at low speed of an electric mixer until smooth. Add egg, and beat at low speed of electric mixer until blended. Beat an additional 3 minutes at medium speed. Stir in remaining 1½ cups flour and raisins.

3 Spoon batter into a 9- x 5- x 3-inch loafpan coated with cooking spray. Cover and let rise in a warm place (85°), free from drafts, 40 minutes or until doubled in bulk.

4 Bake at 350° for 35 to 40 minutes or until golden. Remove from pan, and let cool on a wire rack.

Yield: 18 (½-inch) slices (126 calories per slice).

Hearty Oat and Grain Loaf

Time: Prep 15 minutes; Cook 50 minutes

Per Slice:
Carbohydrate 20.3g
Protein 3.4g
Fat 3.8g
Fiber 2.0g
Cholesterol 12mg
Sodium 132mg
Calcium 70mg
Exchanges
1 Grain
1 Fat

1 cup all-purpose flour
1 cup whole wheat flour
1 cup medium rye flour
1 tablespoon baking powder
½ teaspoon salt
½ cup quick-cooking oats, uncooked
⅓ cup firmly packed brown sugar
1½ cups plus 2 tablespoons skim milk
¼ cup vegetable oil
1 egg, lightly beaten
   Vegetable cooking spray

1 Combine first 7 ingredients in a large bowl; make a well in center of mixture.

2 Combine milk, oil, and egg; add to dry ingredients, stirring just until dry ingredients are moistened.

3 Spoon batter into a 9- x 5- x 3-inch loafpan coated with cooking spray. Bake at 350° for 50 to 55 minutes or until a wooden pick inserted in center comes out clean. Let cool in pan 10 minutes; remove loaf from pan, and let cool completely on a wire rack.

Yield: 18 (½-inch) slices (127 calories per slice).

Desserts

Mocha Fudge Pie (page 110)

Amaretto Fruit Medley

Amaretto Fruit Medley

Time: Prep 20 minutes; Chill 30 minutes

Per Serving:
Carbohydrate 23.3g
Protein 1.6g
Fat 1.6g
Fiber 4.1g
Cholesterol 0mg
Sodium 0mg
Calcium 24mg
Exchanges
1½ Fruit

⅓   cup sliced almonds
3   tablespoons sugar
6   fresh nectarines, pitted and sliced
2   medium oranges, peeled and sectioned
2   fresh plums, pitted and sliced
¼   cup amaretto

1 Combine almonds and sugar in a small nonstick skillet; cook over low heat, stirring constantly, 20 minutes or until sugar melts and coats almonds. Let cool. Break almond mixture into small chunks.

98

2 Place fruit in a large bowl; pour amaretto over fruit mixture, and toss gently. Cover and chill thoroughly. Spoon evenly into 10 compotes. Top evenly with almond mixture.

Yield: 10 servings (117 calories per serving).

Champagne Berry Parfaits

Time: Prep 15 minutes; Cook 30 minutes; Freeze 30 minutes

2	cups fresh strawberries
1	cup champagne
⅓	cup sugar
1½	cups fresh strawberries, halved
1½	cups fresh blackberries
1	cup fresh blueberries
1	cup fresh raspberries
1	quart vanilla nonfat frozen yogurt, softened

Per Serving:
Carbohydrate 40.9g
Protein 4.5g
Fat 0.6g
Fiber 6.5g
Cholesterol 0mg
Sodium 65mg
Calcium 156mg
Exchanges
2½ Fruit
½ Milk

1 Place 2 cups strawberries in container of an electric blender or food processor; cover and process until smooth.

2 Transfer strawberry puree to a saucepan. Add champagne and sugar, stirring well. Bring to a boil; reduce heat, and cook, uncovered, 30 minutes or until mixture is reduced to 1 cup, stirring occasionally.

3 Combine strawberry halves, blackberries, blueberries, and raspberries in a medium bowl. Pour champagne mixture over berries, and toss gently.

4 Spoon ¼ cup yogurt into each of 8 parfait glasses. Top each with ¼ cup berry mixture. Repeat layers with remaining yogurt and berry mixture. Cover and freeze 30 minutes.

Yield: 8 servings (174 calories per serving).

Peach Trifle

Peach Trifle

Time: Prep 25 minutes

<table>
<tr><td>Per Serving:</td><td>1</td><td>(8-ounce) carton vanilla low-fat yogurt</td></tr>
<tr><td>Carbohydrate 50.6g</td><td>1</td><td>(3.4-ounce) package vanilla instant pudding mix</td></tr>
<tr><td>Protein 5.5g</td><td>2</td><td>cups skim milk</td></tr>
<tr><td>Fat 0.6g</td><td>⅓</td><td>cup strawberry jam</td></tr>
<tr><td>Fiber 0.4g</td><td>1</td><td>tablespoon dry sherry</td></tr>
<tr><td>Cholesterol 3mg</td><td>8</td><td>ounces angel food cake, cut into ¾-inch cubes and divided</td></tr>
<tr><td>Sodium 185mg</td><td>2</td><td>cups canned sliced peaches in juice, drained and divided</td></tr>
<tr><td>Calcium 154mg</td><td></td><td>Fresh sliced strawberries (optional)</td></tr>
<tr><td>Exchanges</td><td></td><td>Fresh mint sprigs (optional)</td></tr>
<tr><td>2 Fruit</td><td></td><td></td></tr>
<tr><td>1½ Grain</td><td></td><td></td></tr>
</table>

1 Spoon yogurt onto several layers of heavy-duty paper towels; spread to ½-inch thickness. Cover with additional paper towels; let stand 5 minutes. Scrape yogurt into a bowl, using a rubber spatula.

2 Combine pudding mix and milk, stirring with a wire whisk until blended. Stir drained yogurt into pudding mixture; set aside.

3 Combine jam and sherry, stirring with a wire whisk until blended; set aside.

4 Arrange half of cake cubes in a 2-quart trifle bowl. Spread half of pudding mixture over cake cubes. Drizzle jam mixture evenly over pudding. Arrange 1 cup of sliced peaches over jam mixture. Repeat layering procedure with remaining cake, pudding, and peaches. If desired, garnish with sliced strawberries and mint sprigs.

Yield: 8 servings (226 calories per serving).

Fresh Fruit Mélange with Strawberry Sauce

Time: Prep 15 minutes; Chill 30 minutes

2	fresh ripe peaches, peeled and sliced
2	tablespoons lemon juice
	Strawberry Sauce
2	cups diced fresh pineapple
2	medium kiwifruit, peeled and cut into ¼-inch slices
1	cup fresh strawberries, halved

Per Serving:
Carbohydrate 33.5g
Protein 1.3g
Fat 0.7g
Fiber 4.2g
Cholesterol 0mg
Sodium 3mg
Calcium 25mg
Exchanges
2 Fruit

1 Combine peaches and lemon juice in a small bowl; toss gently.

2 Spoon Strawberry Sauce evenly onto 6 dessert plates. Arrange peaches, pineapple, kiwifruit, and strawberries over sauce. Serve immediately.

Yield: 6 servings (135 calories per serving).

Strawberry Sauce

2	cups fresh strawberries
2	tablespoons sugar
¼	cup red currant jelly

1 Position knife blade in food processor bowl; add strawberries and sugar. Process 1 to 2 minutes or until smooth; set aside.

2 Melt jelly in a small saucepan over medium heat, stirring constantly. Add pureed strawberry mixture, stirring well. Cover, and chill thoroughly. Yield: 1⅔ cups.

Pineapple-Orange Frozen Yogurt

Time: Prep 10 minutes; Freeze 25 minutes

Per Serving:
Carbohydrate 13.4g
Protein 2.6g
Fat 0.1g
Fiber 0.2g
Cholesterol 1mg
Sodium 26mg
Calcium 69mg
Exchanges
½ Fruit
½ Grain

1	envelope unflavored gelatin
¼	cup cold water
2	(8-ounce) cartons plain nonfat yogurt
1	(6-ounce) can frozen orange juice concentrate, thawed and undiluted
1	(8-ounce) can pineapple chunks in juice, drained
⅓	cup sugar
¾	cup cold water
	Fresh raspberries (optional)

1 Sprinkle gelatin over ¼ cup cold water in a small saucepan; let stand 1 minute. Cook over low heat, stirring until gelatin dissolves, about 2 minutes.

2 Place gelatin mixture, yogurt, and next 4 ingredients in container of an electric blender; cover and process until smooth, stopping once to scrape down sides.

3 Pour mixture into freezer can of a 4-quart hand-turned or electric freezer. Freeze according to manufacturer's instructions. Let ripen 1 hour, if desired. Scoop frozen yogurt into individual dessert bowls. Garnish with fresh raspberries, if desired. Serve immediately.

Yield: 14 (½-cup) servings (64 calories per serving).

"When served with an attractive garnish, low-fat desserts can be just as festive and just as satisfying as higher-fat alternatives. Remember to learn to love what's best for you." — Jenny

Blackberry Frozen Yogurt

Blackberry Frozen Yogurt

Time: Prep 15 minutes; Chill at least 2 hours; Freeze 25 minutes

Per Serving:
Carbohydrate 37.8g
Protein 3.2g
Fat 0.7g
Fiber 4.5g
Cholesterol 2mg
Sodium 54mg
Calcium 118mg
Exchanges
2 Fruit
½ Grain

3   cups fresh blackberries
½   cup sugar
1   tablespoon cornstarch
1   cup skim milk
¼   cup light-colored corn syrup
1   cup plain low-fat yogurt
    Fresh blackberries (optional)
    Fresh mint sprigs (optional)

1 Place 3 cups blackberries in container of an electric blender or food processor; cover and process 45 seconds or until smooth. Transfer to a wire-mesh strainer; press with back of spoon against the sides of strainer to squeeze out juice. Discard seeds and pulp in strainer.

2 Combine sugar and cornstarch in a small saucepan. Add milk; bring to a boil, and cook, stirring constantly, 1 minute. Remove from heat. Stir in blackberry puree and corn syrup. Cool completely.

3 Combine blackberry mixture and yogurt in a bowl, stirring well. Cover and chill thoroughly.

4 Pour mixture into freezer can of a 2-quart hand-turned or electric freezer. Freeze according to manufacturer's instructions. Let stand 1 hour, if desired. Scoop into individual dessert bowls. If desired, garnish with blackberries and mint sprigs. Serve immediately.

Yield: 7 (½-cup) servings (165 calories per serving).

Pink Lemonade Ice Milk Cake

Time: Prep 35 minutes; Freeze at least 4 hours

1   (16-ounce) round angel food cake
3   cups low-fat vanilla ice cream, softened
½   cup plus 1 tablespoon frozen pink lemonade concentrate, unthawed
1   cup chopped fresh strawberries

1 Slice cake horizontally into 3 layers; set aside.

2 Combine ice cream, lemonade concentrate, and strawberries; stir well.

3 Place bottom layer of angel food cake in an 8-inch tube pan; spread half of ice cream mixture over cake, and top with middle layer of cake. Freeze 30 minutes. Spread remaining ice cream mixture over middle layer of cake, and top with remaining cake layer. Cover and freeze 4 hours or until firm. Slice into wedges.

Yield: 16 servings (129 calories per serving).

Per Serving:
Carbohydrate 27.8g
Protein 2.6g
Fat 1.2g
Fiber 0.3g
Cholesterol 3mg
Sodium 62mg
Calcium 62mg
Exchanges
1 Fruit
1 Grain

Applesauce Spice Cupcakes

Applesauce Spice Cupcakes

Time: Prep 15 minutes; Cook 16 minutes

Per Cupcake:		
Carbohydrate 27.2g	3	cups sifted cake flour
Protein 2.2g	2½	teaspoons baking powder
Fat 3.1g	1	teaspoon baking soda
Fiber 0.2g	½	teaspoon salt
Cholesterol 0mg	1½	cups sugar
Sodium 119mg	½	teaspoon ground ginger
Calcium 40mg	½	cup frozen egg substitute, thawed
Exchanges	½	cup skim milk
1 Fruit	⅓	cup vegetable oil
1 Grain	1½	cups cinnamon applesauce
1 Fat	2	teaspoons vanilla extract
	3	egg whites
	2	teaspoons powdered sugar
	⅛	teaspoon ground cinnamon

1 Combine first 6 ingredients in a large bowl; make a well in center of mixture.

2 Combine egg substitute, milk, and oil; add to dry ingredients, stirring just until moistened. Stir in applesauce and vanilla.

3 Beat egg whites at high speed of an electric mixer until stiff peaks form. Gently fold beaten egg white into applesauce mixture.

4 Spoon batter into paper-lined muffin pans, filling each three-fourths full. Bake at 400° for 16 to 18 minutes or until a wooden pick inserted in center comes out clean. Remove from pans immediately, and let cool completely on wire racks. Combine powdered sugar and cinnamon; sift over cupcakes.

Yield: 2 dozen (145 calories each).

Warm Gingerbread

Time: Prep 10 minutes; Cook 25 minutes

1½	**cups all-purpose flour**
1	**teaspoon baking soda**
⅛	**teaspoon salt**
¼	**cup sugar**
1½	**teaspoons ground ginger**
1	**teaspoon cinnamon**
¼	**teaspoon ground cloves**
⅔	**cup unsweetened applesauce**
⅓	**cup molasses**
3	**tablespoons vegetable oil**
1	**egg, lightly beaten**
	Vegetable cooking spray

Per Serving:
Carbohydrate 22.5g
Protein 2.1g
Fat 4.0g
Fiber 0.7g
Cholesterol 18mg
Sodium 103mg
Calcium 26mg
Exchanges
½ Fruit
1 Grain
1 Fat

1 Combine first 7 ingredients; stir well.

2 Combine applesauce, molasses, oil, and egg in a small bowl; add to flour mixture, stirring well.

3 Spoon batter into 9-inch square baking pan coated with cooking spray. Bake at 350° for 25 minutes until a wooden pick inserted in center comes out clean. Serve warm.

Yield: 12 servings (133 calories per serving).

Chocolate Espresso Pudding Cake

Time: Prep 10 minutes; Cook 30 minutes

Per Serving:
Carbohydrate 26.8g
Protein 2.3g
Fat 4.9g
Fiber 0g
Cholesterol 1mg
Sodium 88mg
Calcium 75mg
Exchanges
2 Grain
1 Fat

1	cup sifted cake flour
1½	teaspoons baking powder
½	teaspoon baking soda
½	cup sugar
2	tablespoons unsweetened cocoa
1	tablespoon instant espresso powder
½	cup evaporated skimmed milk
¼	cup vegetable oil
1	teaspoon vanilla extract
½	cup firmly packed dark brown sugar
3	tablespoons unsweetened cocoa
2	teaspoons instant espresso powder
1	cup boiling water

1 Combine first 6 ingredients in a bowl; stir well. Combine milk, oil, and vanilla; add to dry ingredients, and stir. Spoon into an 8-inch square pan.

2 Combine brown sugar, 3 tablespoons cocoa, and 2 teaspoons espresso powder. Sprinkle over batter. Pour water over batter. (Do not stir.) Bake at 350° for 30 minutes or until cake springs back when touched. Serve warm.

Yield: 12 servings (161 calories per serving).

Frozen Margarita Pie

Time: Prep 15 minutes; Freeze 1½ hours

Per Serving:
Carbohydrate 34.5g
Protein 5.1g
Fat 3.8g
Fiber 0g
Cholesterol 0mg
Sodium 263mg
Calcium 163mg
Exchanges
2 Grain
1 Fat

2½	cups small pretzels, finely crushed
¼	cup reduced-calorie margarine, melted
1	tablespoon sugar
6	cups vanilla nonfat frozen yogurt, softened
¼	cup tequila
3	tablespoons frozen limeade concentrate, thawed and undiluted
1	teaspoon grated fresh lime rind
1	tablespoon fresh lime juice
	Lime slices and rind curls (optional)
	Edible flowers (optional)

1 Combine first 3 ingredients in a small bowl, stirring well. Press mixture into bottom and up sides of a 9-inch pieplate. Freeze crust 1 hour.

2 Combine yogurt and next 4 ingredients in a bowl, stirring well. Spoon yogurt mixture into prepared crust. Cover and freeze until firm. Let stand at room temperature 5 minutes before slicing. If desired, garnish with lime slices, lime rind curls, and edible flowers.

Yield: 10 servings (198 calories per serving).

Frozen Margarita Pie

Mocha Fudge Pie

Time: Prep 20 minutes; Cook 22 minutes

Per Serving:
Carbohydrate 41.2g
Protein 3.5g
Fat 5.6g
Fiber 0g
Cholesterol 1mg
Sodium 276mg
Calcium 38mg
Exchanges
2½ Grain
1 Fat

⅓ cup hot water
4 teaspoons instant coffee granules, divided
½ (19.85-ounce) box light fudge brownie mix (about 2 cups)
2 teaspoons vanilla extract, divided
2 egg whites
  Vegetable cooking spray
¾ cup 1% low-fat milk
3 tablespoons Kahlúa or other coffee-flavored liqueur, divided
1 (3.9-ounce) package chocolate-flavored instant pudding-and-pie
    filling mix
3 cups frozen reduced-calorie whipped topping, thawed and divided
  Chocolate curls (optional)

1 Combine hot water and 2 teaspoons coffee granules in a medium bowl, stirring well. Add brownie mix, 1 teaspoon vanilla, and egg whites; stir until well blended.

2 Pour mixture into a 9-inch pieplate coated with cooking spray. Bake at 325° for 22 minutes. Let cool completely.

3 Combine milk, 2 tablespoons Kahlúa, 1 teaspoon coffee granules, remaining 1 teaspoon vanilla, and pudding mix in a bowl; beat at medium speed of an electric mixer 1 minute. Gently fold in 1½ cups whipped topping. Spread pudding mixture evenly over brownie crust.

4 Combine remaining 1 tablespoon Kahlúa and remaining 1 teaspoon coffee granules in a bowl, stirring well. Gently fold in remaining 1½ cups whipped topping. Spread whipped topping mixture evenly over pudding mixture. Garnish with chocolate curls, if desired. Serve immediately, or store loosely covered in refrigerator.

Yield: 10 servings (234 calories per serving).

Chocolate-Cherry Squares

Time: Prep 5 minutes; Freeze 1 hour

1	cup diced, pitted fresh sweet cherries
2	tablespoons rum
6	cups low-fat chocolate ice cream, softened
	Vegetable cooking spray
2	teaspoons grated semisweet chocolate

1 Gently fold cherries and rum into ice cream. Spread mixture evenly into an 8-inch square pan coated with cooking spray. Cover and freeze until firm.

2 Sprinkle with grated chocolate, and cut into squares. Serve immediately.

Yield: 9 servings (147 calories per serving).

Per Serving:
Carbohydrate 22.6g
Protein 3.7g
Fat 4.1g
Fiber 0.4g
Cholesterol 12mg
Sodium 70mg
Calcium 218mg
Exchanges
½ Fruit
1 Grain
1 Fat

Steps to Success

Lack of time is probably the most common excuse for avoiding exercise. Here are a few suggestions for working in a workout.

• Take the slow-but-steady approach, especially in the beginning. Overdoing it (hopping on a bicycle every night after a few months of inactivity) is the surest route to burnout, not to mention injury.

• Start in the morning. Many people are tired at the end of the day and use this as an excuse for not exercising. Studies show that three out of four people who work out in the early morning stick with the regimen. Only one out of four afternoon or evening exercisers stay with a program for the long haul.

• Have fun! Pick an activity that you enjoy. Otherwise, chances are slim that you'll stick with it.

Key West Lime Parfaits

Time: Prep 20 minutes; Freeze 1 hour

	Vegetable cooking spray
¼	cup finely chopped macadamia nuts
½	cup plus 2 tablespoons chocolate wafer cookie crumbs, divided
3	cups lime sherbet, softened
1	tablespoon grated lime rind

Per Serving:
Carbohydrate 30.1g
Protein 1.9g
Fat 6.6g
Fiber 0.1g
Cholesterol 8mg
Sodium 104mg
Calcium 53mg
Exchanges
2 Grain
1 Fat

1 Coat a 1-quart casserole with cooking spray. Spread nuts in casserole, and microwave, uncovered, at HIGH 6 to 7 minutes or until lightly toasted, stirring every 30 seconds. Combine nuts and ½ cup cookie crumbs; stir well.

2 Combine lime sherbet and lime rind; stir well.

3 Spoon 1 tablespoon cookie crumb mixture into each of 6 (6-ounce) parfait glasses; top each with ¼ cup sherbet mixture. Spoon 1 tablespoon crumb mixture over each; top each with ¼ cup sherbet mixture. Sprinkle each serving with 1 teaspoon cookie crumbs. Cover and freeze until firm.

Yield: 6 servings (181 calories per serving).

"By dancing in the rain, Gene Kelly unknowingly showed us the wonderful benefits of combining water and exercise. Go ahead, take a dip, make a splash, and above all, have fun with it." — Jenny

Key West Lime Parfaits

Peanut Butter Swirl Brownies

Peanut Butter Swirl Brownies

Time: Prep 22 minutes; Cook 25 minutes

Per Brownie:
Carbohydrate 28.1g
Protein 3.2g
Fat 4.5g
Fiber 0.4g
Cholesterol 0mg
Sodium 151mg
Calcium 29mg
Exchanges
1½ Grain
1 Fat

¼   cup plus 2 tablespoons reduced-calorie stick margarine, melted
1¼ cups firmly packed brown sugar
½   cup frozen egg substitute, thawed
1   teaspoon vanilla extract
1½ cups all-purpose flour
½   teaspoon baking powder
½   teaspoon salt
2   tablespoons unsweetened cocoa
¼   cup 25% less-fat creamy peanut butter
    Vegetable cooking spray

1 Combine margarine and brown sugar in a medium bowl; add egg substitute. Beat at medium speed of an electric mixer until thoroughly combined. Add vanilla; beat well.

2 Combine flour, baking powder, and salt; add to sugar mixture, stirring well.

3 Divide batter in half. Stir cocoa into 1 half; stir peanut butter into other half. (Peanut butter mixture will be thick.)

4 Spoon dollops of each batter alternately into a 9-inch square pan coated with cooking spray. Cut through batters in pan with a knife to create a swirled pattern. Bake at 350° for 25 minutes or until a wooden pick inserted in center comes out clean. Remove from oven, and let cool completely on a wire rack.

Yield: 16 brownies (162 calories each).

Lemon Soufflé Bars

Time: Prep 25 minutes; Cook 33 minutes

¼	cup margarine, softened
⅓	cup sugar
1	egg white
½	teaspoon vanilla extract
1¼	cups all-purpose flour
⅛	teaspoon salt
	Vegetable cooking spray
1	(8-ounce) carton frozen egg substitute, thawed
1	cup sugar
½	cup all-purpose flour
½	teaspoon baking powder
1	tablespoon freshly grated lemon rind
⅓	cup lemon juice
2	teaspoons powdered sugar

Per Bar:
Carbohydrate 12.6g
Protein 1.4g
Fat 1.3g
Fiber 0.2g
Cholesterol 0mg
Sodium 34mg
Calcium 8mg
Exchange
1 Grain

1 Beat margarine at medium speed of an electric mixer until creamy; gradually add ⅓ cup sugar, beating well. Add egg white and vanilla, beating well.

2 Combine 1¼ cups flour and salt; add to margarine mixture, stirring well. Pat into bottom of a 13- x 9- x 2-inch baking dish coated with cooking spray. Bake at 375° for 15 minutes or until lightly browned.

3 Combine egg substitute and 1 cup sugar; beat at medium speed until blended. Combine ½ cup flour and baking powder. Add flour mixture, lemon rind, and lemon juice to egg substitute mixture; stir well. Pour over baked crust.

4 Bake at 350° for 18 to 20 minutes or until set. Let cool completely on a wire rack. Sprinkle with powdered sugar. Cut into bars.

Yield: 3 dozen (67 calories per bar).

Vanilla Cookies

Time: Prep 15 minutes; Freeze 1 hour; Cook 6 minutes

Per Cookie:
Carbohydrate 5.2g
Protein 0.5g
Fat 1.0g
Fiber 0.1g
Cholesterol 0mg
Sodium 30mg
Calcium 3mg
Exchange
½ Grain

⅓ cup margarine, softened
⅔ cup sugar
¼ cup frozen egg substitute, thawed
2 teaspoons vanilla extract
2 cups plus 1 tablespoon all-purpose flour
½ teaspoon baking soda
¼ teaspoon salt
¾ cup crisp rice cereal
   Vegetable cooking spray

1 Beat margarine at medium speed of an electric mixer until creamy; gradually add sugar, beating well. Add egg substitute and vanilla; beat well.

2 Combine flour, soda, and salt. Gradually add flour mixture to creamed mixture; mix well. Stir in cereal.

3 Divide dough into 2 equal portions; place each portion on a sheet of plastic wrap, and shape into an 8- x 1½-inch log. Wrap logs in plastic wrap, and freeze until firm.

4 Unwrap logs, and cut into ¼-inch slices. Place 1 inch apart on cookie sheets coated with cooking spray. Bake at 350° for 6 to 8 minutes or until lightly browned. Remove from cookie sheets, and let cool on wire racks.

Yield: 64 cookies (32 calories each).

Meatless Main Dishes

Goat Cheese Tostadas (page 118)

Goat Cheese Tostadas

Time: Prep 20 minutes; Chill at least 2 hours; Cook 12 minutes

Tomato-Mango Salsa
Vegetable cooking spray
1 teaspoon olive oil
1 cup chopped purple onion
1 teaspoon chili powder
½ teaspoon ground cumin
2 (16-ounce) cans white kidney beans, drained
1 (4-ounce) can chopped green chiles, drained
2 tablespoons lime juice
8 (6-inch) corn tortillas
5 ounces goat cheese, crumbled
3½ cups shredded arugula
3½ cups torn Bibb lettuce
½ cup chopped fresh cilantro
½ cup nonfat sour cream

1 Prepare Tomato-Mango Salsa.

2 Coat a medium saucepan with cooking spray; add oil. Place over medium-high heat until hot. Add onion, chili powder, and cumin; sauté 3 minutes or until onion is tender. Add beans, chiles, and lime juice; stir well. Reduce heat to low, and cook until mixture is heated, mashing beans slightly with a potato masher or wooden spoon. Set aside, and keep warm.

3 Place tortillas on a baking sheet coated with cooking spray. Bake at 350° for 6 minutes; turn tortillas over, and bake an additional 6 minutes or until tortillas are crisp.

4 Place 1 tortilla on each individual serving plate. Spoon bean mixture over tortillas; top with cheese. Combine arugula and cilantro; sprinkle over cheese. Top with sour cream. Serve with Tomato-Mango Salsa.

Yield: 8 servings (236 calories per serving).

Tomato-Mango Salsa

¾ cup seeded, diced tomato
½ cup peeled, diced ripe mango
¼ cup diced purple onion
¼ cup chopped fresh cilantro
2 tablespoons lime juice
1½ teaspoons seeded, minced jalapeño pepper

1 Combine all ingredients in a small bowl. Cover and chill at least 2 hours.
Yield: 1½ cups.

Spinach-Filled Tortilla Rolls

Time: Prep 30 minutes; Cook 30 minutes

2 (14½-ounce) cans no-salt-added whole tomatoes, undrained
1 cup minced fresh basil
1 (10-ounce) package frozen chopped spinach, thawed and drained
1 (15-ounce) carton lite ricotta cheese
2 eggs, lightly beaten
¼ teaspoon salt
6 (8-inch) flour tortillas
  Vegetable cooking spray
¼ cup freshly grated Parmesan cheese

Per Serving:
Carbohydrate 29.0g
Protein 16.0g
Fat 7.5g
Fiber 2.2g
Cholesterol 87mg
Sodium 298mg
Calcium 289mg
Exchanges
1 Vegetable
1½ Grain
1½ Medium-Fat Meat

1 Position knife blade in food processor bowl; add tomato. Pulse 6 to 8 times
or until tomato is coarsely pureed.

2 Transfer tomato to a medium saucepan; add basil. Bring to a boil; reduce
heat, and simmer 25 minutes, stirring frequently.

3 Combine spinach, ricotta cheese, eggs, and salt; stir well. Spoon spinach
mixture evenly down centers of tortillas. Roll up tortillas; place seam side
down in a 13- x 9- x 2-inch baking dish coated with cooking spray. Spoon
tomato mixture over tortillas, and sprinkle with Parmesan cheese. Bake at
375° for 30 minutes or until thoroughly heated.

Yield: 6 servings (234 calories per serving).

Corn, Zucchini, and Black-Eyed Pea Quesadillas

Corn, Zucchini, and Black-Eyed Pea Quesadillas

Time: Prep 15 minutes; Cook 8 minutes

Per Serving:
Carbohydrate 26.9g
Protein 13.8g
Fat 8.7g
Fiber 5.3g
Cholesterol 19mg
Sodium 425mg
Calcium 275mg
Exchanges
1 Vegetable
2 Grain
1 Lean Meat
1 Fat

1	cup seeded, diced tomato
½	cup water
¼	cup peeled, diced avocado
2½	tablespoons minced fresh cilantro
2	tablespoons minced purple onion
1	tablespoon seeded, minced jalapeño pepper
2	tablespoons fresh lime juice
¼	teaspoon ground cumin
⅛	teaspoon garlic powder
	Vegetable cooking spray
1	cup julienne-sliced zucchini
1	cup frozen whole kernel corn, thawed
1	cup canned black-eyed peas, drained
4	(8-inch) flour tortillas
¾	cup (3 ounces) shredded reduced-fat Cheddar cheese
¾	cup (3 ounces) shredded reduced-fat Monterey Jack cheese
	Fresh cilantro sprigs (optional)

1 Combine first 9 ingredients in a medium bowl; stir well. Set aside.

2 Coat a large nonstick skillet with cooking spray; place over medium-high heat until hot. Add zucchini; sauté 3 minutes or until tender. Add corn and peas; sauté 2 minutes.

3 Place 2 tortillas on a baking sheet coated with cooking spray; top tortillas with cheeses and zucchini mixture. Top with remaining tortillas. Bake at 400° for 8 minutes or just until tortillas are crisp and cheese melts. Cut each into thirds. Place on individual serving plates; top with tomato mixture. Garnish with cilantro sprigs, if desired.

Yield: 6 servings (234 calories per serving).

Vegetable Risotto in a Bag

Time: Prep 15 minutes; Cook 1 hour

1	tablespoon all-purpose flour
3	cups shredded fresh spinach
1	cup diced sweet red pepper
1	cup sliced fresh mushrooms
1	cup sliced green onions
⅔	cup Arborio or other short-grain rice, uncooked
2	cloves garlic, minced
1	(10½-ounce) can low-sodium chicken broth, undiluted
1	(14-ounce) can cannellini beans, drained
¾	cup dry white wine
½	teaspoon dried basil
1	cup freshly grated Parmesan cheese
¼	teaspoon freshly ground pepper

Per Serving:
Carbohydrate 29.1g
Protein 11.8g
Fat 5.4g
Fiber 2.9g
Cholesterol 13mg
Sodium 469mg
Calcium 268mg
Exchanges
2 Grain
1 Medium-Fat Meat

1 Add flour to a large oven cooking bag; twist end to close, and shake to coat inside. Add spinach and next 5 ingredients; squeeze to blend ingredients. Add chicken broth, beans, wine, and basil; squeeze bag gently to distribute ingredients in a single layer. Secure bag with an ovenproof tie or string.

2 Place bag in a 13- x 9- x 2-inch pan. Cut six ½-inch slits in top of bag. Bake at 350° for 1 hour or until rice is tender and mixture is creamy. Transfer rice mixture to a serving dish; stir in cheese and ground pepper.

Yield: 6 servings (216 calories per serving).

Mediterranean Pita Rounds

Mediterranean Pita Rounds

Time: Prep 10 minutes; Cook 11 minutes

Per Serving:	2 (15-ounce) cans no-salt-added garbanzo beans, drained
Carbohydrate 64.8g	¼ cup skim milk
Protein 13.5g	¼ cup fresh lemon juice
Fat 6.6g	5 cloves garlic
Fiber 11.9g	8 (8-inch) pita bread rounds
Cholesterol 6mg	1 teaspoon olive oil
Sodium 602mg	1 (10-ounce) package frozen chopped spinach, thawed and drained
Calcium 196mg	2 cups chopped tomato
Exchanges	1 cup diced green pepper
1 Vegetable	1 cup diced sweet red pepper
4 Grain	½ cup crumbled feta cheese
1 Fat	⅓ cup sliced ripe olives

1 Position knife blade in food processor bowl; add first 4 ingredients. Process until smooth, scraping sides of processor bowl occasionally. Set aside.

2 Arrange pita bread rounds on ungreased baking sheets; brush with olive oil. Bake at 450° for 6 minutes.

3 Spread bean mixture evenly over pitas, leaving a ½-inch border. Arrange spinach and remaining ingredients evenly over pita rounds.

4 Bake at 450° for 5 minutes or until thoroughly heated and crust is crisp.

Yield: 8 servings (379 calories per serving).

Chile Cheese Puff

Time: Prep 10 minutes; Cook 50 minutes

	Vegetable cooking spray
1	**(4-ounce) can chopped green chiles, drained**
½	**cup sliced fresh mushrooms**
½	**cup chopped onion**
2	**cups nonfat cottage cheese**
1	**cup frozen egg substitute, thawed**
1	**cup (4 ounces) shredded part-skim mozzarella cheese**
½	**cup (2 ounces) shredded reduced-fat Monterey Jack cheese**
¼	**cup all-purpose flour**
2	**tablespoons reduced-calorie margarine, melted**
1	**teaspoon baking powder**
⅛	**teaspoon salt**
4	**egg whites**

Per Serving:

Carbohydrate 7.4g
Protein 18.3g
Fat 5.5g
Fiber 0.4g
Cholesterol 15mg
Sodium 509mg
Calcium 226mg
Exchanges
2 Vegetable
2 Lean Meat

1 Coat a 2-quart casserole with cooking spray. Layer green chiles, mushrooms, and onion in casserole; set aside.

2 Position knife blade in food processor bowl; add cottage cheese and remaining ingredients. Process until smooth, scraping sides of processor bowl once. Spoon cheese mixture over vegetables in prepared casserole.

3 Bake at 350° for 50 to 55 minutes or until set. Let stand 10 minutes before serving.

Yield: 8 servings (151 calories per serving).

Corn Frittata

Corn Frittata

Time: Prep 10 minutes; Cook 20 minutes

Per Serving:
Carbohydrate 11.2g
Protein 13.7g
Fat 4.3g
Fiber 1.9g
Cholesterol 12mg
Sodium 295mg
Calcium 194mg
Exchanges
2 Vegetable
1½ Lean Meat

Vegetable cooking spray
1¼ cups fresh corn cut from cob (about 3 ears)
¼ cup chopped green onions
1½ cups frozen egg substitute, thawed
⅓ cup skim milk
1½ teaspoons minced fresh basil
⅛ teaspoon salt
⅛ teaspoon pepper
2 small tomatoes, cut into 12 wedges
1 cup (4 ounces) shredded reduced-fat Cheddar cheese
Fresh basil sprigs (optional)

1 Coat a medium nonstick skillet with cooking spray; place over medium-high heat until hot. Add corn and green onions; sauté until tender.

2 Combine egg substitute and next 4 ingredients; stir well. Pour egg mixture over vegetables in skillet. Cover and cook over medium-low heat 15 minutes or until mixture is almost set.

3 Arrange tomato wedges near center of egg mixture, and sprinkle with

Cheddar cheese. Cover and cook 5 additional minutes or until cheese melts. Cut frittata into 6 wedges. Garnish with fresh basil sprigs, if desired. Serve immediately.

Yield: 6 servings (133 calories per serving).

Mexican Potato Ragoût

Time: Prep 25 minutes; Cook 45 minutes

1	pound round red potatoes, quartered
1	tablespoon olive oil, divided
2	cups diced onion
3	tablespoons chopped garlic
	Vegetable cooking spray
2	cups cubed eggplant
2	cups cubed zucchini
1	cup coarsely chopped green pepper
1	(15-ounce) can garbanzo beans, drained
4	plum tomatoes, cut into thin wedges
½	cup minced fresh cilantro
2	teaspoons dried oregano
1	teaspoon grated lemon rind
½	teaspoon ground cumin
¼	teaspoon salt
1½	cups (6 ounces) shredded nonfat Monterey Jack cheese

Per Serving:
Carbohydrate 38.2g
Protein 14.0g
Fat 4.1g
Fiber 5.8g
Cholesterol 5mg
Sodium 401mg
Calcium 288mg
Exchanges
2 Vegetable
2 Grain
½ Lean Meat
½ Fat

1 Cook potato in boiling water to cover 10 to 15 minutes or just until tender. Drain and set aside.

2 Heat 1 teaspoon olive oil in a large nonstick skillet over medium-high heat. Add onion and garlic; sauté 5 minutes. Transfer to a 13- x 9- x 2-inch baking dish coated with cooking spray.

3 Add remaining 2 teaspoons olive oil to skillet; add eggplant, zucchini, and pepper; cook over medium heat 5 minutes, stirring frequently. Transfer to baking dish; add beans and next 6 ingredients, stirring well.

4 Cover and bake at 350° for 30 minutes. Stir in potato; sprinkle with cheese. Bake, uncovered, 15 additional minutes or until thoroughly heated.

Yield: 6 servings (245 calories per serving).

Vegetarian Chili

Time: Prep 15 minutes; Stand 1 hour; Cook 37 minutes

Per Serving:

Carbohydrate 40.2g
Protein 10.3g
Fat 2.1g
Fiber 6.8g
Cholesterol 0mg
Sodium 279mg
Calcium 82mg
Exchanges
2 Grain
2 Vegetable
1 Lean Meat

2	(14½-ounce) cans no-salt-added stewed tomatoes, undrained
¾	cup bulgur (cracked wheat), uncooked
1	teaspoon olive oil
1½	cups chopped green pepper
1¼	cups chopped onion
1	cup chopped celery
1	cup chopped carrot
4	cloves garlic, minced
¼	cup plus 1 tablespoon chili powder
1	tablespoon fresh lemon juice
1	teaspoon dried basil
1	teaspoon dried oregano
1	teaspoon ground cumin
1	teaspoon pepper
½	teaspoon salt
2	(15-ounce) cans kidney beans, drained
1	(15-ounce) can no-salt-added garbanzo beans (chick-peas), drained
3	cups no-salt-added tomato juice

1 Drain stewed tomatoes, reserving juice. Pour 1 cup reserved stewed tomato juice into a small saucepan; bring to a boil. Add bulgur. Remove from heat. Cover, and let stand 1 hour or until bulgur is tender and liquid is absorbed. Set aside.

2 Heat oil in a large Dutch oven over medium-high heat until hot. Add green pepper, onion, celery, carrot, and garlic; sauté until tender. Stir in drained stewed tomatoes, chili powder and next 6 ingredients. Cook, stirring constantly, 1 minute. Stir in remaining stewed tomato juice, bulgur mixture, kidney beans, garbanzo beans, and no-salt-added tomato juice.

3 Bring to a boil; reduce heat, and simmer, uncovered, 30 minutes, stirring occasionally. Ladle into soup bowls. Serve immediately.

Yield: 11 (1-cup) servings (205 calories per serving).

Capellini with Cilantro Pesto

Time: Prep 5 minutes; Cook 15 minutes

1½	cups firmly packed fresh cilantro
1½	cups firmly packed fresh flat-leaf parsley
2	tablespoons water
1½	tablespoons fresh lime juice
1	tablespoon olive oil
¼	teaspoon salt
3	cloves garlic, halved
8	ounces capellini (angel hair pasta), uncooked
½	cup freshly grated Romano cheese
3	tablespoons chopped walnuts, lightly toasted

Per Serving:
Carbohydrate 46.1g
Protein 13.7g
Fat 11.0g
Fiber 2.6g
Cholesterol 15mg
Sodium 334mg
Calcium 200mg
Exchanges
3 Grain
½ High-Fat Meat
1 Fat

1 Position knife blade in food processor bowl; add first 7 ingredients. Process until smooth, scraping sides of processor bowl occasionally.

2 Cook pasta according to package directions, omitting salt and fat; drain.

3 Place pasta in a serving bowl. Add cilantro mixture, Romano cheese, and walnuts; toss gently. Serve immediately.

Yield: 4 (1-cup) servings (337 calories per serving).

"My good friend, Georgia Leonard, introduced me to her vegetarian chili a few years ago, and it's become one of my all-time favorite one-dish meals. I hope it becomes yours too. It's satisfying, simple, and simply delicious."— Jenny

Linguine with Asparagus and Goat Cheese

Time: Prep 15 minutes; Cook 15 minutes

Per Serving:
Carbohydrate 40.2g
Protein 11.5g
Fat 8.8g
Fiber 2.5g
Cholesterol 27mg
Sodium 237mg
Calcium 98mg
Exchanges
2 Vegetable
2 Grain
2 Fat

½ pound fresh asparagus
½ cup canned no-salt-added chicken broth, undiluted
¼ cup dry white wine
¼ cup chopped shallots
¼ teaspoon pepper
½ (8-ounce) package Neufchâtel cheese, softened
2 ounces goat cheese, crumbled
2 tablespoons fresh lemon juice
8 ounces linguine, uncooked
½ cup thinly sliced sweet red pepper

1 Snap off tough ends of asparagus. Remove scales from stalks with a knife or vegetable peeler, if desired. Cut asparagus into 1-inch pieces. Set aside.

2 Combine broth, wine, shallots, and ¼ teaspoon pepper in a saucepan. Bring to a boil; add asparagus. Reduce heat, and simmer 5 minutes. Add cheeses and lemon juice; cook over low heat, stirring constantly, until cheeses melt. Set aside, and keep warm.

3 Cook pasta according to package directions, omitting salt and fat; drain. Place pasta in a serving bowl. Add asparagus mixture and sweet red pepper; toss gently. Serve immediately.

Yield: 5 (1-cup) servings (284 calories per serving).

Meats, Poultry & Seafood

Holiday Turkey Cutlets (page 149)

Beef Tenderloin with Horseradish Sauce

Time: Prep 5 minutes; Cook 35 minutes

Per Serving:
Carbohydrate 3.1g
Protein 20.2g
Fat 6.0g
Fiber 0.2g
Cholesterol 54mg
Sodium 75mg
Calcium 45mg
Exchanges
3 Lean Meat

1	(8-ounce) carton nonfat sour cream
¼	cup minced fresh parsley
¼	cup prepared horseradish
1	teaspoon white wine Worcestershire sauce
⅛	teaspoon pepper
1	(2-pound) beef tenderloin
½	teaspoon salt-free lemon-pepper seasoning
	Vegetable cooking spray

1 Combine first 5 ingredients. Cover and chill.

2 Trim fat from tenderloin. Sprinkle lemon-pepper seasoning over tenderloin; place on a rack in a roasting pan coated with cooking spray. Insert meat thermometer into thickest part of tenderloin, if desired. Bake at 500° for 35 minutes or until thermometer registers 145° (medium-rare) or 160° (medium). Let stand 10 minutes before slicing. Serve with sauce.

Yield: 8 servings (155 calories per serving).

Marinated Beef Kabobs

Time: Prep 20 minutes; Marinate 4 hours; Cook 12 minutes

Per Serving:
Carbohydrate 5.9g
Protein 29.0g
Fat 6.2g
Fiber 1.5g
Cholesterol 73mg
Sodium 179mg
Calcium 23mg
Exchanges
4 Lean Meat

½	cup red wine vinegar
¼	cup water
¼	cup low-sodium soy sauce
1½	teaspoons sugar
½	teaspoon dried thyme
¼	teaspoon freshly ground pepper
1	clove garlic, crushed
1	pound top round steak, cut into 1½-inch pieces
8	medium-size fresh mushrooms
1	large yellow squash, cut into ½-inch pieces
1	medium-size green pepper, seeded and cut into 1-inch pieces
	Vegetable cooking spray
8	cherry tomatoes

1 Combine first 7 ingredients in a heavy-duty, zip-top plastic bag. Add steak; seal bag, and shake until steak is well coated. Marinate in refrigerator 4 to 8 hours, turning bag occasionally.

2 Remove steak from marinade; reserve marinade. Thread steak, mushrooms, squash, and pepper alternately on 4 (15-inch) skewers. Bring marinade to a boil in a saucepan. Reduce heat, and simmer 3 minutes.

3 Coat grill rack with cooking spray; place on grill over medium-hot coals (350° to 400°). Place kabobs on rack; grill, covered, 6 minutes on each side or to desired degree of doneness, basting frequently with marinade. Add tomatoes to skewers during last 1 minute of cooking.

Yield: 4 servings (198 calories per serving).

Marinated Beef Kabobs

Grilled Sirloin with Citrus Salsa

Grilled Sirloin with Citrus Salsa

Time: Prep 20 minutes; Marinate 2 hours; Cook 10 minutes

1½ pounds lean boneless top sirloin steak
½ cup low-sodium soy sauce
¼ cup chopped green onions
2 tablespoons dark brown sugar
3 tablespoons fresh lime juice
⅛ teaspoon hot sauce
1 clove garlic, minced
Vegetable cooking spray
Citrus Salsa

1 Trim fat from steak. Place steak in a dish. Combine soy sauce and next 5 ingredients. Pour over steak, turning to coat. Marinate in refrigerator 2 hours.

2 Remove steak from marinade. Coat grill rack with cooking spray; place on grill over medium-hot coals. Place steak on rack; grill, covered, 5 minutes on each side or to desired degree of doneness. Let steak stand 5 minutes. Cut diagonally across grain into slices; arrange on serving plates. Serve with Citrus Salsa.

Yield: 6 servings (200 calories per serving).

Citrus Salsa

2   oranges, peeled, seeded, and chopped
½   teaspoon grated lemon rind
½   teaspoon grated lime rind
½   small lemon, peeled, seeded, and finely chopped
½   small lime, peeled, seeded, and finely chopped
¼   cup chopped green onions
1   tablespoon sugar
1   tablespoon chopped fresh cilantro
1   teaspoon seeded, minced jalapeño pepper
⅛   teaspoon salt
2   tablespoons unsweetened orange juice
2   tablespoons rice vinegar

1 Combine all ingredients in a small bowl. Cover and chill at least 2 hours. Yield: 1¼ cups.

Marinated Flank Steak

Time: Prep 5 minutes; Marinate 8 hours; Cook 10 minutes

1   (1½-pound) lean flank steak
½   cup sliced green onions
1   tablespoon sugar
2   tablespoons peeled, grated gingerroot
2   tablespoons low-sodium soy sauce
2   tablespoons dry sherry
2   cloves garlic, minced
    Vegetable cooking spray

Per Serving:
Carbohydrate 1.5g
Protein 20.4g
Fat 12.1g
Fiber 0g
Cholesterol 56mg
Sodium 154mg
Calcium 5mg
Exchanges
3 Medium-Fat Meat

1 Trim fat from steak. Score steak on both sides. Combine green onions and next 5 ingredients in a shallow dish; add steak, turning to coat with marinade. Cover and marinate in refrigerator 8 hours; turn occasionally.

2 Remove steak from marinade; discard marinade. Place steak on rack of a broiler pan coated with cooking spray. Broil 5½ inches from heat 5 to 7 minutes on each side or to desired degree of doneness.

3 Slice steak diagonally across grain into ¼-inch slices.

Yield: 6 servings (204 calories per serving).

Veal Patties Marsala

Time: Prep 15 minutes; Cook 15 minutes

Per Serving:
Carbohydrate 5.0g
Protein 25.2g
Fat 5.5g
Fiber 1.3g
Cholesterol 88mg
Sodium 75mg
Calcium 30mg
Exchanges
1 Vegetable
3 Lean Meat

1½ **pounds ground veal**
½ **teaspoon pepper**
  Vegetable cooking spray
1 **(8-ounce) package presliced fresh mushrooms**
½ **cup sliced green onions**
1½ **cups peeled, seeded, and chopped tomato**
⅓ **cup Marsala**
2 **tablespoons chopped fresh parsley**

1 Combine veal and pepper in a medium bowl; stir well. Shape mixture into 6 (¾-inch-thick) patties.

2 Coat a large nonstick skillet with cooking spray; place over medium-high heat until hot. Add veal patties, and cook 5 minutes on each side or to desired degree of doneness. Remove patties from skillet; drain and pat dry with paper towels. Wipe drippings from skillet with a paper towel.

3 Coat skillet with cooking spray; place over medium-high heat until hot. Add mushrooms, and sauté until tender. Transfer to a bowl, and set aside.

4 Coat skillet with cooking spray; place over medium-high heat until hot. Add green onions, and sauté 2 minutes. Stir in tomato and Marsala. Bring to a boil; reduce heat, and simmer, uncovered, 5 minutes. Stir in mushrooms. Return veal patties to skillet, and spoon mushroom mixture over patties. Cover and cook over low heat until thoroughly heated. Transfer patties and mushroom mixture to a serving platter, and sprinkle with parsley. Serve immediately.

Yield: 6 servings (173 calories per serving).

Easy Veal Milano

Time: Prep 15 minutes; Cook 10 minutes

1	pound veal cutlets (¼ inch thick)
3	tablespoons all-purpose flour
¼	teaspoon salt
¼	teaspoon pepper
	Vegetable cooking spray
1	teaspoon olive oil
1	cup sliced fresh mushrooms
2	cloves garlic, minced
1	(14½-ounce) can no-salt-added whole tomatoes, undrained and crushed
3	tablespoons sliced ripe olives
¼	teaspoon dried basil
2	cups cooked linguine (cooked without salt or fat)

Per Serving:
Carbohydrate 31.4g
Protein 28.5g
Fat 6.3g
Fiber 2.0g
Cholesterol 94mg
Sodium 337mg
Calcium 72mg
Exchanges
1 Vegetable
2 Grain
3 Lean Meat

1 Trim fat from cutlets; cut cutlets into 2-inch pieces. Combine flour, salt, and pepper; dredge veal pieces in flour mixture.

2 Coat a nonstick skillet with cooking spray; add olive oil. Place over medium-high heat until hot. Add veal, and cook 2 minutes on each side or until browned. Remove from skillet; set aside, and keep warm.

3 Coat skillet with cooking spray, and place over medium-high heat until hot. Add mushrooms and garlic; sauté until tender. Stir in tomato, olives, and basil; cook over high heat 3 minutes. Return veal to skillet; cover, reduce heat, and simmer 5 minutes. Serve over pasta.

Yield: 4 servings (299 calories per serving).

"I use a lot of herbs and spices in my cooking to make up for the lack of fat—and I never miss it. Spices add a world of flavor and almost no calories. Try this ethnic treat for a taste of sunny Italy."— Jenny

Teriyaki Lamb Chops

Time: Prep 10 minutes; Marinate 8 hours; Cook 14 minutes

Per Serving:
Carbohydrate 14.6g
Protein 26.6g
Fat 8.8g
Fiber 0g
Cholesterol 84mg
Sodium 471mg
Calcium 31mg
Exchanges
1 Grain
3 Lean Meat

4   (5-ounce) lean lamb loin chops (1 inch thick)
½   cup dry sherry
¼   cup firmly packed brown sugar
¼   cup low-sodium soy sauce
2   tablespoons water
1   tablespoon peeled, minced gingerroot
     Vegetable cooking spray

1 Trim fat from chops. Place chops in a large heavy-duty, zip-top plastic bag. Combine sherry and next 4 ingredients; stir well. Pour over chops; seal bag, and shake until chops are well coated. Marinate in refrigerator 8 hours, turning bag occasionally.

2 Remove chops from marinade. Place marinade in a small saucepan. Bring to a boil; reduce heat, and simmer 2 minutes.

3 Coat grill rack with cooking spray; place on grill over medium-hot coals (350° to 400°). Place chops on rack; grill, uncovered, 7 to 9 minutes on each side or to desired degree of doneness, basting occasionally with marinade.

Yield: 4 servings (257 calories per serving).

Grilled Lamb Chops

Time: Prep 10 minutes; Marinate 8 hours; Cook 14 minutes

Per Serving:
Carbohydrate 14.8g
Protein 26.8g
Fat 9.0g
Fiber 0.1g
Cholesterol 84mg
Sodium 84mg
Calcium 28mg
Exchanges
1 Fruit
3 Lean Meat

4   (5-ounce) lean lamb loin chops (1 inch thick)
½   cup frozen apple juice concentrate, thawed and undiluted
½   teaspoon curry powder
½   teaspoon ground cumin
¼   teaspoon garlic powder
     Vegetable cooking spray

1 Trim fat from chops. Place chops in a large heavy-duty, zip-top plastic bag. Combine apple juice concentrate and next 3 ingredients; stir well. Pour over chops; seal bag, and shake until chops are well coated. Marinate in refrigerator 8 hours, turning bag occasionally.

2 Remove lamb from marinade. Place marinade in a small saucepan. Bring to a boil; reduce heat, and simmer 5 minutes.

3 Coat grill rack with cooking spray; place on grill over medium-hot coals (350° to 400°). Place chops on rack, and grill, uncovered, 7 to 9 minutes on each side or to desired degree of doneness, basting chops frequently with marinade.

Yield: 4 servings (253 calories per serving).

Grilled Lamb Chops

Sweet-and-Sour Pork

Sweet-and-Sour Pork

Time: Prep 20 minutes; Cook 30 minutes

<table>
<tr><td>

Per Serving:
Carbohydrate 43.6g
Protein 21.5g
Fat 6.3g
Fiber 1.5g
Cholesterol 56mg
Sodium 98mg
Calcium 36mg
Exchanges
1 Fruit
1 Vegetable
1½ Grain
2 Lean Meat

</td><td>

1½ pounds lean boneless pork loin
   Vegetable cooking spray
1 (8-ounce) can no-salt-added tomato sauce
¼ cup cider vinegar
2 tablespoons brown sugar
2 teaspoons low-sodium soy sauce
⅛ teaspoon garlic powder
⅛ teaspoon pepper
1 (20-ounce) can pineapple chunks in juice, undrained
1 medium-size green pepper, seeded and cut into 1-inch pieces
1 small onion, thinly sliced
2 tablespoons cornstarch
4 cups cooked long-grain rice (cooked without salt or fat)

</td></tr>
</table>

1 Trim fat from pork; cut into ½-inch pieces. Coat a large nonstick skillet with cooking spray; place over medium-high heat until hot. Add pork; cook 10 minutes or until browned, stirring frequently. Remove pork from skillet; drain and pat dry with paper towels. Wipe drippings from skillet with a paper towel.

2 Return pork to skillet, and add tomato sauce and next 5 ingredients; bring to a boil. Cover, reduce heat, and simmer 15 minutes or until pork is tender.

3 Drain pineapple, reserving juice; add enough water to juice to equal 1 cup. Set aside. Add pineapple, green pepper, and onion to skillet; cover and simmer 5 to 7 minutes or until vegetables are crisp-tender.

4 Combine cornstarch and pineapple juice mixture; stir into pork mixture. Cook, stirring constantly, until thickened and bubbly. Serve over rice.

Yield: 8 servings (322 calories per serving).

Sesame Pork Brochettes

Time: Prep 15 minutes; Marinate 2 hours; Cook 8 minutes

1½	**pounds lean boneless pork loin (½ inch thick)**
¼	**cup honey**
2	**tablespoons sesame seeds, toasted and divided**
3	**tablespoons lemon juice**
1	**tablespoon low-sodium soy sauce**
¾	**teaspoon ground cumin**
½	**teaspoon ground cinnamon**
	Vegetable cooking spray
3	**cups cooked couscous (cooked without salt or fat)**

Per Serving:
Carbohydrate 33.4g
Protein 31.4g
Fat 10.4g
Fiber 0.5g
Cholesterol 83mg
Sodium 134mg
Calcium 23mg
Exchanges
2 Grain
3 Lean Meat

1 Trim fat from pork; cut pork into ¼-inch-wide strips. Place pork in a shallow dish. Combine honey, 1½ tablespoons sesame seeds, and next 4 ingredients in container of an electric blender; cover and process until smooth. Pour over pork. Cover and marinate in refrigerator 2 hours.

2 Remove pork from marinade, reserving marinade. Thread pork onto 12 (10-inch) skewers. Place skewers on rack of a broiler pan coated with cooking spray. Broil 5½ inches from heat 4 minutes. Turn and baste with reserved marinade; broil 4 additional minutes or until done.

3 Place couscous on a large serving platter. Arrange skewers over couscous, and sprinkle with remaining 1½ teaspoons sesame seeds. Serve immediately.

Yield: 6 servings (357 calories per serving).

Brandy-Pear Pork Tenderloins

Brandy-Pear Pork Tenderloins

Time: Prep 15 minutes; Marinate at least 2 hours; Cook 45 minutes

Per Serving:
Carbohydrate 8.4g
Protein 24.0g
Fat 5.3g
Fiber 1.3g
Cholesterol 71mg
Sodium 55mg
Calcium 26mg
Exchanges
½ Fruit
3 Lean Meat

2   (¾-pound) pork tenderloins
½   cup brandy
⅔   cup finely chopped fresh pear
2   tablespoons finely chopped almonds, toasted
2   tablespoons raisins, chopped
1   tablespoon cider vinegar
2   teaspoons chopped crystallized ginger
    Vegetable cooking spray
    Fresh pear slices (optional)

1 Trim fat from pork. Cut pork lengthwise to within ½ inch of outer edge of each tenderloin, leaving 1 long side connected; flip cut piece over to enlarge tenderloin. Place in a shallow dish; pour brandy over tenderloins, and turn to coat. Cover, and marinate in refrigerator at least 2 hours, turning occasionally.

2 Remove tenderloins from marinade. Place marinade in a small saucepan; bring to a boil. Reduce heat, and simmer 5 minutes.

3 Combine chopped pear and next 4 ingredients; stir well. Spread half of mixture in center of each tenderloin to within ½ inch of sides. Bring sides of meat together, and secure at 2-inch intervals with string.

4 Place tenderloins on a rack in a roasting pan coated with cooking spray. Insert meat thermometer into thickest part of tenderloin, if desired. Bake, uncovered, at 375° for 45 minutes or until meat thermometer registers 160°, basting frequently with marinade. Let stand 10 minutes; slice into 18 slices, and arrange on a large serving platter. Garnish with pear slices, if desired.

Yield: 6 servings (179 calories per serving).

Honey-Mustard Chicken Nuggets

Time: Prep 5 minutes; Cook 14 minutes

1	teaspoon ground coriander
⅛	teaspoon salt
⅛	teaspoon pepper
1	pound unbreaded chicken breast nuggets
	Vegetable cooking spray
¼	cup chopped shallot
1	large clove garlic, minced
½	cup canned low-sodium chicken broth, undiluted
3	tablespoons honey mustard

Per Serving:
Carbohydrate 5.8g
Protein 27.0g
Fat 3.5g
Fiber 0.1g
Cholesterol 72mg
Sodium 239mg
Calcium 24mg
Exchanges
½ Grain
3½ Lean Meat

1 Combine first 3 ingredients; stir well. Add chicken, tossing to coat.

2 Coat a large nonstick skillet with cooking spray; place over medium-high heat until hot. Add shallot and garlic; sauté 1 minute. Add chicken, and cook 10 minutes or until chicken is tender, stirring frequently. Remove chicken from skillet; drain on paper towels. Wipe drippings from skillet with a paper towel.

3 Add broth and mustard to skillet; cook over medium heat, stirring constantly, 3 minutes or until thickened and bubbly. Add chicken; cook until thoroughly heated.

Yield: 4 servings (169 calories per serving).

Lemon-Dijon Chicken Breasts

Time: Prep 5 minutes; Cook 30 minutes

Per Serving:
Carbohydrate 7.9g
Protein 27.4g
Fat 2.3g
Fiber 0.4g
Cholesterol 66mg
Sodium 300mg
Calcium 35mg
Exchanges
½ Grain
3½ Lean Meat

½ cup fine, dry breadcrumbs
2 teaspoons grated lemon rind
3 tablespoons lemon juice
2 tablespoons country-style Dijon mustard
1 tablespoon lime juice
6 (4-ounce) skinned, boned chicken breast halves
Vegetable cooking spray
Lemon slices (optional)

1 Combine breadcrumbs and lemon rind, stirring well. Combine lemon juice, mustard, and lime juice; brush over both sides of chicken.

2 Dredge chicken in breadcrumb mixture. Place chicken in a 13- x 9- x 2-inch baking dish coated with cooking spray; sprinkle with any remaining breadcrumb mixture.

3 Bake, uncovered, at 375° for 15 minutes. Turn chicken, and bake 15 additional minutes or until done. Garnish with lem   slices, if desired.

Yield: 6 servings (170 calories per serving).

Quick Sesame-Ginger Chicken

Time: Prep 5 minutes; Cook 8 minutes

Per Serving:
Carbohydrate 9.1g
Protein 26.3g
Fat 4.3g
Fiber 0.1g
Cholesterol 70mg
Sodium 258mg
Calcium 16mg
Exchanges
½ Grain
3 Lean Meat

1½ tablespoons sesame seeds, toasted
1 tablespoon grated fresh gingerroot
3 tablespoons low-sodium soy sauce
3 tablespoons honey
6 (4-ounce) skinned, boned chicken breast halves
Vegetable cooking spray

1 Combine first 4 ingredients; set aside.

2 Place chicken between 2 sheets of heavy-duty plastic wrap, and flatten to ¼-inch thickness, using a meat mallet or rolling pin. Brush half of soy sauce mixture over chicken, coating both sides.

3 Coat grill rack with cooking spray; place on grill over medium-hot coals. Place chicken on rack, and grill, covered, 8 to 10 minutes or until chicken is done, turning and basting frequently with remaining soy sauce mixture.

Yield: 6 servings (187 calories per serving).

Chicken Breasts with Feta Cheese Sauce

Time: Prep 4 minutes; Cook 14 minutes

Vegetable cooking spray
6 (4-ounce) skinned, boned chicken breast halves
1 tablespoon margarine
1 tablespoon plus 1 teaspoon all-purpose flour
1 (12-ounce) can evaporated skimmed milk
1 tablespoon freeze-dried chives
¾ cup (3 ounces) crumbled feta cheese

Per Serving:
Carbohydrate 8.3g
Protein 32.9g
Fat 8.2g
Fiber 0g
Cholesterol 87mg
Sodium 309mg
Calcium 248mg
Exchanges
½ Skim Milk
4 Lean Meat

1 Coat a large nonstick skillet with cooking spray; place over medium heat until hot. Add chicken, and cook 7 minutes on each side or until done; set aside, and keep warm.

2 Melt margarine in a small saucepan over medium heat; add flour. Cook 1 minute, stirring constantly with a wire whisk. Gradually add milk, stirring constantly. Stir in chives. Reduce heat to medium-low, and cook, stirring constantly, 3 minutes or until thickened and bubbly. Add cheese, and stir until cheese melts. Spoon over chicken.

Yield: 6 servings (246 calories per serving).

"Because of its sharp flavor, a small amount of feta cheese goes a long way. You can store leftover feta in the freezer for future use—just thaw it in the refrigerator before using."—Jenny

Herbed Chicken with Mushroom Pesto

Time: Prep 15 minutes; Cook 30 minutes

Per Serving:
Carbohydrate 8.3g
Protein 26.8g
Fat 2.0g
Fiber 0.1g
Cholesterol 64mg
Sodium 384mg
Calcium 34mg
Exchanges
½ Grain
3½ Lean Meat

1   cup loosely packed fresh basil leaves
¾   cup sliced fresh mushrooms
4   cloves garlic
2   tablespoons nonfat buttermilk
6   (6-ounce) skinned chicken breast halves
     Vegetable cooking spray
3   tablespoons low-sodium soy sauce
2   tablespoons honey
½   teaspoon dark sesame oil

1 Position knife blade in food processor bowl; add first 3 ingredients. Process 3 seconds or until blended. Slowly add buttermilk through food chute with processor running, blending until mixture forms a paste.

2 Place 1 chicken breast, bone side down, on a cutting board; cut lengthwise into side of breast, forming a pocket. Stuff pocket with one-sixth of mushroom mixture. Place chicken, breast side up, on a rack in a roasting pan coated with cooking spray. Repeat procedure with remaining chicken breasts and mushroom mixture.

3 Combine soy sauce, honey, and sesame oil; brush over chicken. Bake at 400° for 30 minutes or until chicken is tender and golden, basting occasionally.

Yield: 6 servings (162 calories per serving).

Thai Chicken Barbecue

Time: Prep 5 minutes; Marinate at least 4 hours; Cook 20 minutes

½   cup firmly packed brown sugar
½   cup low-sodium soy sauce
2   tablespoons fresh lime juice
6   cloves garlic, minced
1   teaspoon crushed red pepper
¾   teaspoon curry powder
2   (3-pound) broiler-fryers, cut up and skinned
    Vegetable cooking spray

Per Serving:
Carbohydrate 9.7g
Protein 23.7g
Fat 6.1g
Fiber 0.1g
Cholesterol 73mg
Sodium 333mg
Calcium 24mg
Exchanges
½ Grain
3 Lean Meat

1 Combine first 6 ingredients in an extra-large heavy-duty, zip-top plastic bag; add chicken. Seal bag, and marinate in refrigerator at least 4 hours, turning occasionally.

2 Remove chicken from marinade, reserving marinade. Place marinade in a small saucepan; bring to a boil. Reduce heat, and simmer 3 minutes.

3 Coat grill rack with cooking spray; place on grill over medium-hot coals. Place chicken on rack, and grill, covered, 20 to 25 minutes or until chicken is done, turning and basting frequently with marinade.

Yield: 12 servings (197 calories per serving).

Fork-Tender Results

Marinades with acidic ingredients such as vinegar, wine, citrus juices, and yogurt provide flavor and help tenderize lean cuts of meat. But don't marinate too long—some red meats can marinate to mush, and poultry and fish can become tough. Be sure to follow each recipe for fork-tender results.

Turkey Tostadas

Time: Prep 15 minutes; Cook 15 minutes

Per Serving:
Carbohydrate 25.1g
Protein 18.0g
Fat 5.5g
Fiber 1.6g
Cholesterol 41mg
Sodium 264mg
Calcium 118mg
Exchanges
2 Grain
2 Lean Meat

6	(6-inch) flour tortillas
	Vegetable cooking spray
¾	pound freshly ground raw turkey
¼	cup minced onion
2	cloves garlic, minced
1	jalapeño pepper, seeded and minced
1	(8-ounce) can no-salt-added tomato sauce
¾	cup chopped tomato
1	teaspoon dried oregano
½	teaspoon dried thyme
	Dash of hot sauce
⅓	cup (1.3 ounces) shredded reduced-fat sharp Cheddar cheese
¼	cup plus 2 tablespoons nonfat sour cream

1 Place tortillas on a baking sheet; bake at 350° for 7 to 10 minutes or until crisp. Set aside.

2 Coat a large nonstick skillet with cooking spray; place over medium-high heat until hot. Add turkey and next 3 ingredients; cook until meat is browned, stirring to crumble. Drain; wipe drippings from skillet with a paper towel.

3 Return turkey mixture to skillet, and add tomato sauce and next 4 ingredients. Bring to a boil; reduce heat, and simmer 10 minutes or until thickened, stirring occasionally.

4 Spoon turkey mixture evenly over tortillas; sprinkle evenly with cheese. Broil 5½ inches from heat until cheese melts. Top with sour cream.

Yield: 6 servings (225 calories per serving).

Holiday Turkey Cutlets

Time: Prep 10 minutes; Cook 15 minutes

1	pound turkey cutlets, cut into 8 pieces
3	tablespoons all-purpose flour
2	teaspoons vegetable oil
¾	cup chopped onion
¾	cup fresh cranberries
½	cup canned low-sodium chicken broth, undiluted
2	tablespoons sugar
2	tablespoons red wine vinegar
2	tablespoons commercial fat-free Catalina dressing
¼	teaspoon salt
	Fresh sage sprigs (optional)
	Orange slices (optional)

Per Serving:
Carbohydrate 15.7g
Protein 27.5g
Fat 4.1g
Fiber 0.5g
Cholesterol 68mg
Sodium 295mg
Calcium 19mg
Exchanges
1 Fruit
4 Lean Meat

1 Place cutlets between 2 sheets of heavy-duty plastic wrap, and flatten to ⅛-inch thickness, using a meat mallet or rolling pin. Dredge cutlets in flour.

2 Heat oil in a large nonstick skillet over medium heat until hot. Add cutlets, and cook 2 minutes on each side or until browned. Transfer to a platter, and keep warm. Wipe drippings from skillet with a paper towel.

3 Place skillet over medium-high heat until hot. Add onion, and sauté until tender. Add cranberries and next 5 ingredients; bring to a boil. Reduce heat, and simmer 3 to 4 minutes or until cranberries pop. Spoon over cutlets, and serve immediately. If desired, garnish with sage sprigs and orange slices.

Yield: 4 servings (218 calories per serving).

"Garnished with fresh sage and orange slices, this quick dish can be more festive than traditional fare which has three times the fat. 'Tis the season to be healthy!"—Jenny

Turkey Scallopini

Time: Prep 6 minutes; Cook 6 minutes

4   (4-ounce) turkey cutlets
3   tablespoons freshly grated Parmesan cheese
3   tablespoons Italian-seasoned breadcrumbs
¼   teaspoon freshly ground pepper
    Vegetable cooking spray
1½ teaspoons olive oil
¼   cup dry white wine
2   tablespoons lemon juice
2   tablespoons chopped fresh parsley

1 Place cutlets between 2 sheets of heavy-duty plastic wrap; flatten to ⅛-inch thickness, using a meat mallet or rolling pin.

2 Combine cheese, breadcrumbs, and pepper; dredge cutlets in breadcrumb mixture.

3 Coat a nonstick skillet with cooking spray; add olive oil. Place over medium-high heat until hot. Add cutlets; cook 2 minutes on each side or until browned. Add wine and lemon juice; cook 2 minutes or until heated. Transfer to a serving platter; sprinkle with parsley.

Yield: 4 servings (178 calories per serving).

A Slimmer, Trimmer You

Want to trim inches off just your hips, thighs, or around your middle? Forget it. Spot reducing schemes may be advertised as a way to melt away fat from a particular area, but that's a biologically impossible feat.

The only way to get rid of excess fat is to eat less and exercise more. Fat "melts" away from all over the body no matter what exercise you choose. Fortunately, the areas of greatest fat concentration (hips, thighs, and midriff) are often the first place to show that loss.

Turkey Tetrazzini Toss

Time: Prep 20 minutes; Cook 7 minutes

Vegetable cooking spray
1 (8-ounce) package presliced fresh mushrooms
¼ cup chopped onion
3 tablespoons all-purpose flour
1 cup canned no-salt-added chicken broth, undiluted
1 cup evaporated skimmed milk
1 cup frozen English peas, thawed
3 tablespoons dry sherry
¼ teaspoon salt
⅛ teaspoon pepper
8 ounces vermicelli, uncooked
2 cups shredded cooked turkey breast
2 tablespoons diced pimiento, drained
3 tablespoons freshly grated Parmesan cheese

Per Serving:

Carbohydrate 37.0g
Protein 23.7g
Fat 2.3g
Fiber 2.5g
Cholesterol 40mg
Sodium 242mg
Calcium 164mg
Exchanges
1 Vegetable
2 Grain
2 Lean Meat

1 Coat a large nonstick skillet with cooking spray; place over medium-high heat until hot. Add mushrooms and onion; sauté 3 minutes or until tender.

2 Combine flour and chicken broth, stirring with a wire whisk until smooth. Gradually add broth mixture to mushroom mixture, stirring constantly. Cook over medium heat, stirring constantly, 2 minutes or until thickened and bubbly.

3 Gradually stir in milk and next 4 ingredients; cook over low heat 2 minutes or until thoroughly heated, stirring frequently.

4 Cook pasta according to package directions, omitting salt and fat; drain.

5 Place pasta in a serving bowl. Add mushroom mixture, turkey, and pimiento; toss well. Sprinkle with cheese. Serve immediately.

Yield: 7 servings (269 calories per serving).

Grilled Amberjack with Pepper-Corn Salsa

Time: Prep 17 minutes; Cook 8 minutes

Per Serving:
Carbohydrate 16.8g
Protein 28.6g
Fat 7.6g
Fiber 3.2g
Cholesterol 43mg
Sodium 153mg
Calcium 14mg
Exchanges
1 Fruit
4 Lean Meat

1	cup fresh corn cut from cob (about 2 ears)
1	(7-ounce) jar roasted red peppers in water, drained and diced
½	cup peeled, diced ripe papaya
¼	cup minced fresh cilantro
1	teaspoon olive oil
½	teaspoon freshly ground pepper
4	(4-ounce) amberjack or yellowtail steaks (¾ inch thick)
1	tablespoon low-sodium soy sauce
	Vegetable cooking spray

1 Place corn on a baking sheet; bake at 450° for 12 minutes, stirring occasionally. Transfer to a bowl. Add peppers and next 4 ingredients.

2 Brush steaks with soy sauce. Coat grill rack with cooking spray; place on grill over hot coals. Place steaks on rack; grill, covered, 4 minutes on each side or until fish flakes easily when tested with a fork. Serve with pepper mixture.

Yield: 4 servings (247 calories per serving).

Grouper with Roasted Ratatouille

Time: Prep 15 minutes; Cook 37 minutes

Per Serving:
Carbohydrate 12.9g
Protein 17.6g
Fat 1.7g
Fiber 4.0g
Cholesterol 28mg
Sodium 161mg
Calcium 88mg
Exchanges
2 Vegetable
2 Lean Meat

1	(1-pound) eggplant
1	medium-size sweet red pepper
1	medium-size sweet yellow pepper
1	medium zucchini
2	small yellow squash
1	cup chopped sweet onion
2	cloves garlic, minced
	Olive oil-flavored vegetable cooking spray
2	teaspoons minced fresh rosemary
¼	teaspoon salt
2	(8-ounce) grouper fillets, cut into 1½-inch pieces
½	cup seeded, diced plum tomato
1	tablespoon balsamic vinegar
½	teaspoon freshly ground pepper
¼	pound fresh spinach leaves

1 Peel eggplant; cut eggplant and peppers into 1-inch pieces. Cut zucchini and squash lengthwise in quarters; cut into 1-inch pieces.

2 Combine eggplant, sweet peppers, zucchini, squash, onion, and garlic in a 15- x 10- x 1-inch jellyroll pan, and coat with cooking spray; toss gently. Sprinkle minced rosemary and salt over vegetable mixture; toss gently. Bake at 400° for 25 minutes or until tender, stirring occasionally.

3 Add grouper; bake 12 additional minutes or until fish flakes easily when tested with a fork. Drain well.

4 Combine tomato, vinegar, and ground pepper. Add to fish mixture; toss gently.

5 Arrange spinach leaves on individual serving plates; spoon fish mixture over spinach.

Yield: 6 servings (132 calories per serving).

Grouper with Roasted Ratatouille

Roasted Halibut and Onions

Time: Prep 5 minutes; Cook 45 minutes

Per Serving:
Carbohydrate 10.3g
Protein 24.9g
Fat 6.2g
Fiber 2.1g
Cholesterol 53mg
Sodium 211mg
Calcium 90mg
Exchanges
2 Vegetable
3 Lean Meat

3	medium-size purple onions, sliced
1	tablespoon olive oil
2	teaspoons dried oregano
1	tablespoon balsamic vinegar
½	teaspoon sugar
¼	teaspoon salt
¼	teaspoon pepper
4	(4-ounce) halibut steaks (¾ inch thick)

1 Combine first 3 ingredients in a 13- x 9- x 2-inch baking dish; toss to coat. Bake, uncovered, at 400° for 35 minutes, stirring occasionally.

2 Add vinegar and next 3 ingredients; stir well. Add halibut steaks to onion mixture; spoon onion mixture evenly over steaks. Bake 10 additional minutes or until fish flakes easily when tested with a fork.

3 Transfer steaks to a serving platter; top evenly with onion mixture.

Yield: 4 servings (200 calories per serving).

Baked Mahimahi with Tomatillo Salsa

Time: Prep 15 minutes; Cook 15 minutes

Per Serving:
Carbohydrate 3.5g
Protein 21.7g
Fat 2.4g
Fiber 0.8g
Cholesterol 84mg
Sodium 254mg
Calcium 14mg
Exchanges
3 Lean Meat

½	cup husked, finely chopped tomatillos
½	cup seeded, finely chopped yellow tomato
¼	cup minced green onions
3	tablespoons minced fresh cilantro
1	tablespoon seeded, minced jalapeño pepper
½	teaspoon ground cumin
¼	teaspoon salt
¼	teaspoon pepper
1½	tablespoons lemon juice
1	teaspoon dark sesame oil
4	(4-ounce) mahimahi fillets
	Olive oil-flavored vegetable cooking spray

1 Combine first 8 ingredients in a small bowl. Cover and chill thoroughly.

2 Combine lemon juice and sesame oil; brush evenly over both sides of fillets. Place fillets in an 11- x 7- x 1½-inch baking dish coated with cooking spray. Bake, uncovered, at 450° for 15 minutes or until fish flakes easily when tested with a fork.

3 Transfer to a serving platter. Spoon tomatillo mixture over fillets. Serve immediately.

Yield: 4 servings (124 calories per serving).

Oriental Red Snapper

Time: Prep 5 minutes; Marinate 30 minutes; Cook 10 minutes

½	cup thinly sliced green onions
1	tablespoon peeled, minced gingerroot
1	teaspoon sugar
¼	teaspoon salt
¼	teaspoon dried crushed red pepper
2	cloves garlic, crushed
2	tablespoons low-sodium soy sauce
2	tablespoons unsweetened pineapple juice
1	teaspoon dark sesame oil
4	(4-ounce) red snapper fillets

Per Serving:
Carbohydrate 4.1g
Protein 23.7g
Fat 2.7g
Fiber 0.4g
Cholesterol 42mg
Sodium 395mg
Calcium 49mg
Exchanges
3 Lean Meat

1 Combine first 9 ingredients; stir well. Place fillets in a shallow dish; spread green onion mixture evenly over fillets. Cover and marinate in refrigerator 30 minutes.

2 Line a vegetable steamer with a plate at least 1 inch smaller in diameter than the steamer. Transfer fillets to plate, using a slotted spoon; discard marinade. Place vegetable steamer over boiling water. Cover and steam 10 minutes or until fish flakes easily when tested with a fork.

Yield: 4 servings (143 calories per serving).

Grilled Herbed Salmon

Grilled Herbed Salmon

Time: Prep 5 minutes; Cook 10 minutes

Per Serving:		
Carbohydrate 4.7g	2	teaspoons cracked pepper
Protein 24.8g	4	(4-ounce) salmon steaks (¾ inch thick)
Fat 10.2g	1	medium onion, thinly sliced
Fiber 1.1g	1	lemon, thinly sliced
Cholesterol 77mg		Vegetable cooking spray
Sodium 60mg	1	bunch fresh thyme (about ½ ounce)
Calcium 20mg		Lemon slices (optional)
Exchanges		Fresh thyme sprigs (optional)
3½ Lean Meat		

1 Press pepper onto both sides of each salmon steak. Top with onion and slices of 1 lemon; set aside.

2 Coat grill rack with cooking spray; place on grill over medium-hot coals. Arrange 1 bunch fresh thyme on grill rack; place salmon on fresh thyme. Grill, covered, 10 minutes or until fish flakes easily when tested with a fork.

3 Transfer steaks to a serving platter, discarding grilled thyme and lemon slices. If desired, garnish with lemon slices and thyme sprigs.

Yield: 4 servings (215 calories per serving).

Tuna Steaks Sicilian

Time: Prep 10 minutes; Cook 40 minutes

	Olive oil-flavored vegetable cooking spray
3	cloves garlic, minced
1	(8-ounce) can no-salt-added tomato sauce
2	cups chopped plum tomatoes (about 4 medium)
¼	cup chopped fresh parsley
½	teaspoon dried oregano
¼	teaspoon crushed red pepper flakes
2	(12-ounce) tuna steaks (1 inch thick)
¼	cup sliced pimiento-stuffed olives
2	tablespoons capers
	Fresh parsley sprigs (optional)

Per Serving:
Carbohydrate 6.5g
Protein 27.6g
Fat 6.3g
Fiber 0.9g
Cholesterol 43mg
Sodium 250mg
Calcium 15mg
Exchanges
1 Vegetable
3½ Lean Meat

1 Coat a large nonstick skillet with cooking spray; place over medium-high heat until hot. Add garlic, and sauté until lightly browned. Add tomato sauce and next 4 ingredients. Reduce heat, and simmer, uncovered, 5 minutes.

2 Spoon half of tomato mixture into an 11- x 7- x 2-inch baking dish; place tuna steaks on tomato mixture. Spoon remaining tomato mixture evenly over steaks. Sprinkle with olives and capers.

3 Cover and bake at 350° for 40 minutes or until fish flakes easily when tested with a fork. Transfer to a serving platter. Garnish with parsley sprigs, if desired.

Yield: 6 servings (197 calories per serving).

Scallops Sauté

Scallops Sauté

Time: Prep 10 minutes; Cook 10 minutes

Per Serving:		
		Vegetable cooking spray
Carbohydrate 14.9g	2	tablespoons reduced-calorie margarine
Protein 22.6g	1	pound fresh Sugar Snap peas
Fat 4.9g	2½	cups diagonally sliced celery
Fiber 4.2g	1	pound fresh sea scallops
Cholesterol 37mg	¼	cup dry white wine
Sodium 306mg	3	tablespoons lemon juice
Calcium 113mg	½	teaspoon dried dillweed
Exchanges	½	teaspoon freshly ground pepper
3 Vegetable	2	tablespoons chopped fresh parsley
2 Lean Meat		

158

1 Coat a large nonstick skillet with cooking spray; add margarine. Place over medium-high heat until margarine melts. Add peas and celery; sauté 3 to 4 minutes or until crisp-tender. Remove vegetables from skillet, using a slotted spoon; set aside.

2 Add scallops and next 4 ingredients to skillet; bring to a boil. Cover, reduce heat, and simmer 5 to 6 minutes or until scallops are opaque.

3 Add vegetables, and cook just until thoroughly heated. Sprinkle with chopped parsley, and serve with a slotted spoon.

Yield: 4 servings (191 calories per serving).

Sweet-and-Sour Shrimp

Time: Prep 20 minutes; Cook 10 minutes

2	cups sliced carrot
1½	cups fresh snow pea pods
2	cups uncooked instant rice
	Vegetable cooking spray
¾	pound medium-size peeled, deveined shrimp
½	cup drained, sliced water chestnuts
1	tablespoon white vinegar
1	(25-ounce) jar sweet-and-sour simmer sauce

Per Serving:
Carbohydrate 73.1g
Protein 16.0g
Fat 1.4g
Fiber 2.6g
Cholesterol 86mg
Sodium 263mg
Calcium 61mg
Exchanges
1 Fruit
2 Vegetable
3 Grain
½ Lean Meat

1 Combine carrot and snow peas in a 1-quart casserole. Cover and microwave at HIGH 5 minutes or until crisp-tender, stirring halfway through cooking time. Drain; set aside.

2 Cook rice according to package directions, omitting salt and fat.

3 Coat a large nonstick skillet with cooking spray, and place over medium-high heat until hot. Add shrimp; stir-fry 3 minutes. Add carrot mixture, water chestnuts, and remaining ingredients; stir well. Cook 1 minute or until thoroughly heated. Serve over rice.

Yield: 6 servings (362 calories per serving).

Chilled Lobster Tails with Mustard Vinaigrette

Time: Prep 30 minutes; Marinate 4 hours; Cook 6 minutes

4	(8-ounce) frozen lobster tails, thawed
¼	cup plus 1 tablespoon dry white wine
1½	tablespoons white wine vinegar
1	tablespoon finely chopped fresh parsley
1	tablespoon Dijon mustard
1	teaspoon chopped fresh dillweed
1	teaspoon olive oil
½	teaspoon sugar
½	teaspoon minced garlic
1	medium cucumber, scored and thinly sliced
	Lemon wedges (optional)

Per Serving:
Carbohydrate 4.7g
Protein 25.2g
Fat 1.5g
Fiber 0.5g
Cholesterol 87mg
Sodium 516mg
Calcium 90mg
Exchanges
1 Vegetable
3 Lean Meat

1 Cook lobster tails in boiling water 6 to 8 minutes or until done; drain. Rinse with cold water.

2 Split lobster tails lengthwise, cutting through upper hard shell with an electric knife. Remove lobster meat through split shell, leaving meat intact. Set shells aside.

3 Score lobster meat at 1-inch intervals. Place lobster in a heavy-duty, zip-top plastic bag. Combine wine and next 7 ingredients; pour over lobster. Seal bag, and marinate in refrigerator 4 hours, turning occasionally.

4 Remove lobster from marinade, reserving marinade. Place reserved shells on individual serving plates. Place lobster meat on shells. Dip cucumber slices in reserved marinade. Place a cucumber slice in each score on lobster. Arrange remaining cucumber slices around tails. Garnish with lemon wedges, if desired.

Yield: 4 servings (145 calories per serving).

Chilled Lobster Tails with Mustard Vinaigrette

Shrimp Alfredo

Time: Prep 10 minutes; Cook 10 minutes

Per Serving:
Carbohydrate 31.2g
Protein 27.1g
Fat 7.3g
Fiber 1.6g
Cholesterol 159mg
Sodium 437mg
Calcium 253mg
Exchanges
2 Grain
3 Lean Meat

6	cups water
2	pounds fresh shrimp, peeled and deveined
1	tablespoon margarine
2	small cloves garlic, minced
1	tablespoon all-purpose flour
1⅓	cups skim milk
2	tablespoons light process cream cheese product
1¼	cups (2½ ounces) grated fresh Parmesan cheese, divided
4	cups hot cooked fettuccine, cooked without salt or fat
2	teaspoons chopped fresh parsley
	Freshly ground pepper

1 Bring water to a boil in a medium saucepan; add shrimp, and cook 3 to 5 minutes or until shrimp turn pink. Drain well. Set aside, and keep warm.

2 Melt margarine in a saucepan over medium heat. Add garlic; sauté 1 minute. Stir in flour.

3 Gradually add milk, stirring with a wire whisk until blended; cook, stirring constantly, 8 minutes or until thickened and bubbly.

4 Stir in cream cheese, cook 2 minutes. Add 1 cup cheese, stirring constantly until it melts.

5 Pour over fettuccine; toss well to coat. Add shrimp; toss gently. Top with remaining ¼ cup Parmesan cheese, parsley, and pepper.

Yield: 6 servings (306 calories per serving).

Salads & Dressings

Baby Greens with Warm Goat Cheese (page 171)

Cantaloupe-Blueberry Salad

Time: Prep 10 minutes; Chill 15 minutes

Per Serving:
Carbohydrate 17.7g
Protein 2.7g
Fat 1.0g
Fiber 2.8g
Cholesterol 1mg
Sodium 30mg
Calcium 70mg
Exchanges
1 Fruit

1	(8-ounce) carton vanilla low-fat yogurt
1	tablespoon lemon juice
1½	teaspoons poppy seeds
1	teaspoon grated orange rind
1	medium cantaloupe, peeled and seeded
24	Boston lettuce leaves
2	cups fresh blueberries

1 Combine first 4 ingredients; stir well. Cover and chill.

2 Cut cantaloupe lengthwise into 32 slices. Arrange 4 slices on each of 8 lettuce-lined serving plates; top each with ¼ cup blueberries. Spoon yogurt mixture over salads.

Yield: 8 servings (83 calories per serving).

Strawberry-Plum Salad Cups

Strawberry-Plum Salad Cups

Time: Prep 10 minutes; Chill 15 minutes

1   (3-inch) vanilla bean, split lengthwise
2   tablespoons sugar
2   cups sliced fresh strawberries
2   medium-size fresh plums, pitted and thinly sliced
    Crisp Salad Shells
    Fresh mint sprigs (optional)

1 Scrape seeds from vanilla bean into a small bowl. Add sugar, stirring until combined.

2 Place strawberries in a bowl; sprinkle sugar mixture over strawberries, and toss gently. Cover and chill until sugar dissolves and mixture is thick. Stir in plum slices.

3 Place Crisp Salad Shells on individual salad plates; spoon strawberry mixture evenly into cups, using a slotted spoon. Garnish with mint sprigs, if desired. Serve immediately.

Yield: 4 servings (198 calories per serving).

Crisp Salad Shells
1   tablespoon hot water
½   teaspoon vanilla extract
4   (6-inch) flour tortillas
    Vegetable cooking spray
1   tablespoon sugar
1   teaspoon ground cinnamon

1 Combine water and vanilla. Coat both sides of each tortilla with cooking spray, and brush with water mixture. Combine sugar and cinnamon; sprinkle over both sides of each tortilla.

2 Place each tortilla in a 6-ounce custard cup, pressing gently in center to form a cup. Bake at 400° for 5 minutes or until lightly browned. Cool completely in custard cups. Yield: 4 salad shells.

Per Serving:
Carbohydrate 42.7g
Protein 3.1g
Fat 3.2g
Fiber 3.8g
Cholesterol 0mg
Sodium 1mg
Calcium 43mg
Exchanges
1 Fruit
1½ Grain
½ Fat

Summer Fruit Salad in Lemonade Glaze

Time: Prep 15 minutes; Chill 3 hours

Per Serving:
Carbohydrate 19.7g
Protein 1.3g
Fat 0.9g
Fiber 2.4g
Cholesterol 0mg
Sodium 3mg
Calcium 18mg
Exchange
1 Fruit

1 (11-ounce) can mandarin oranges in water, undrained
¼ teaspoon unflavored gelatin
¼ cup frozen lemonade concentrate, thawed
1 teaspoon poppy seeds
2 cups fresh cherries, pitted and halved
2 cups sliced fresh peaches
1½ cups sliced fresh plums
Bibb lettuce leaves (optional)

1 Drain oranges, reserving ¼ cup liquid. Combine reserved liquid and gelatin in a small saucepan; let stand 1 minute. Stir in lemonade concentrate. Bring to a boil, and cook 2 minutes or until gelatin dissolves, stirring constantly.

2 Remove from heat, and stir in poppy seeds. Cover and chill 3 hours or until mixture is thickened.

3 Combine oranges, cherries, peaches, and plums; toss gently. Pour lemonade mixture over fruit mixture, and toss gently.

Yield: 6 (1-cup) servings (85 calories per serving).

Colorful Corn Salad

Time: Prep 10 minutes; Chill 3 hours

Per Serving:
Carbohydrate 16.7g
Protein 2.1g
Fat 2.6g
Fiber 1.7g
Cholesterol 0mg
Sodium 155mg
Calcium 18mg
Exchange
1 Grain

1⅔ cups frozen whole kernel corn
1 (4-ounce) jar diced pimiento, drained
½ cup chopped green pepper
¼ cup chopped green onions
1 tablespoon sugar
2 tablespoons cider vinegar
1 teaspoon celery seeds
2 teaspoons vegetable oil
¼ teaspoon salt

1 Cook corn according to package directions, omitting salt. Drain well, and let cool.

2 Combine corn, pimiento, and remaining ingredients in a medium bowl, stirring well. Cover and chill at least 3 hours.

Yield: 4 (½-cup) servings (88 calories per serving).

Summer Fruit Salad in Lemonade Glaze

Minted Cucumber and Tomato Salad

Time: Prep 10 minutes; Chill 10 minutes

Per Serving:
Carbohydrate 5.7g
Protein 2.3g
Fat 0.2g
Fiber 0.8g
Cholesterol 1mg
Sodium 102mg
Calcium 69mg
Exchange
1 Vegetable

1	tablespoon minced fresh mint
¼	teaspoon salt
1	clove garlic, minced
1	(8-ounce) carton plain nonfat yogurt
1	tablespoon lemon juice
2	cups thinly sliced English cucumber
2	cups thinly sliced plum tomato
½	cup fresh cilantro sprigs

1 Combine first 3 ingredients, crushing with a mortar and pestle. Add yogurt and lemon juice; stir well. Cover and chill.

2 Combine cucumber, tomato, and cilantro. Add yogurt mixture, and toss well.

Yield: 8 (½-cup) servings (32 calories per serving).

Chinese Coleslaw

Time: Prep 12 minutes

Per Serving:
Carbohydrate 11.2g
Protein 2.1g
Fat 2.4g
Fiber 1.3g
Cholesterol 0mg
Sodium 161mg
Calcium 42mg
Exchanges
2 Vegetable
½ Fat

2½	cups thinly sliced savoy cabbage
¼	cup coarsely shredded carrot
2	tablespoons thinly sliced green onions
¼	cup seasoned rice vinegar
1	teaspoon sugar
1	tablespoon water
2	teaspoons low-sodium soy sauce
1	teaspoon dark sesame oil
1	clove garlic, minced

1 Combine first 3 ingredients in a bowl.

2 Combine vinegar and remaining ingredients; stir well. Pour over cabbage mixture; toss well.

Yield: 2 (1-cup) servings (68 calories per serving).

Zesty Potato Salad

Time: Prep 5 minutes; Cook 15 minutes; Chill 8 hours

2	pounds small round red potatoes
⅓	cup chopped green onions
¼	cup chopped fresh parsley
1	(10½-ounce) can low-sodium chicken broth, undiluted
¼	cup cider vinegar
2	tablespoons vegetable oil
1	tablespoon coarse-grained mustard
1	teaspoon sugar
¼	teaspoon salt
¼	teaspoon freshly ground pepper

Per Serving:
Carbohydrate 13.8g
Protein 1.9g
Fat 2.4g
Fiber 1.5g
Cholesterol 0mg
Sodium 73mg
Calcium 17mg
Exchange
1 Grain

1 Wash potatoes. Cook in boiling water to cover 15 minutes or until tender; drain and cool. Slice potatoes; place in a bowl, and add onions and parsley.

2 Combine chicken broth and remaining ingredients in a saucepan; bring to a boil. Pour over potato mixture; toss gently. Cover; chill at least 8 hours.

Yield: 12 (½-cup) servings (83 calories per serving).

"When I'm in a hurry, I pull out the food processor to shred vegetables for coleslaw and other salads. This trims preparation to almost seconds."— Jenny

Tomato Salad with Goat Cheese Dressing

Tomato Salad with Goat Cheese Dressing

Time: Prep 10 minutes

Per Serving:
Carbohydrate 11.3g
Protein 7.1g
Fat 3.1g
Fiber 2.9g
Cholesterol 10mg
Sodium 298mg
Calcium 75mg
Exchanges
1 Vegetable
1 Lean Meat

6	(¼-inch-thick) slices unpeeled yellow or red tomato
4	large Boston lettuce leaves
2	tablespoons skim milk
1½	tablespoons chèvre (mild goat cheese)
1	tablespoon nonfat sour cream
1	teaspoon chopped fresh thyme
⅛	teaspoon salt
	Freshly ground pepper

1 Arrange tomato slices on 2 lettuce-lined salad plates.

2 Combine milk and next 4 ingredients, stirring well with a wire whisk. Spoon over salads; sprinkle with pepper.

Yield: 2 servings (90 calories per serving).

Baby Greens with Warm Goat Cheese

Time: Prep 12 minutes; Cook 3 minutes

3	tablespoons water
1½	tablespoons sherry vinegar
1	teaspoon walnut oil
¾	teaspoon dry mustard
5	cups mixed baby salad greens
2	tablespoons minced fresh parsley
1	teaspoon minced shallots
2	tablespoons finely chopped walnuts
2	ounces goat cheese, cut into 4 slices
	Vegetable cooking spray

Per Serving:
Carbohydrate 2.6g
Protein 3.5g
Fat 6.5g
Fiber 0.9g
Cholesterol 13mg
Sodium 200mg
Calcium 96mg
Exchanges
1 Vegetable
1 Fat

1 Combine first 4 ingredients in a small bowl; stir with a wire whisk until blended. Set aside.

2 Combine greens, parsley, and shallots in a medium bowl; add vinegar mixture, and toss well.

3 Lightly press chopped walnuts into both sides of each cheese slice. Place cheese slices on a baking sheet coated with cooking spray. Bake at 425° for 3 minutes.

4 Arrange greens evenly on individual salad plates. Place 1 cheese slice on each salad plate. Serve immediately.

Yield: 4 servings (85 calories per serving).

Mixed Greens with Tangelo Vinaigrette

Mixed Greens with Tangelo Vinaigrette

Time: Prep 20 minutes

Per Serving:	2 teaspoons coarse-grained mustard
Carbohydrate 27.0g	2 teaspoons sherry vinegar
Protein 2.5g	1 teaspoon grated tangelo rind
Fat 0.7g	5 tangelos
Fiber 7.5g	1 tablespoon honey
Cholesterol 0mg	1½ cups loosely packed watercress leaves
Sodium 58mg	1½ cups arugula
Calcium 86mg	1 cup thinly sliced Belgian endive
Exchanges	1 pint fresh strawberries, sliced
1½ Fruit	
1 Vegetable	**1** Combine first 3 ingredients in a small jar, and set aside.

2 Peel and section 2 tangelos; set aside. Squeeze juice from remaining 3 tangelos to measure ½ cup juice. Combine juice and honey in a small saucepan, stirring well. Bring juice mixture to a boil; cook, uncovered, until reduced to ⅓ cup, stirring occasionally. Remove from heat, and cool completely. Add juice mixture to mustard mixture in jar; cover tightly, and shake vigorously.

3 Combine watercress, arugula, and endive in a bowl; add mustard mixture, and toss gently. Place watercress mixture evenly on individual salad plates; top with tangelo sections and strawberry slices.

Yield: 4 servings (115 calories per serving).

Caesar Salad

Time: Prep 15 minutes

4   (½-inch-thick) slices French bread
     Butter-flavored vegetable cooking spray
½   teaspoon garlic powder
6   cups torn romaine lettuce
2   tablespoons freshly grated Parmesan cheese
3½   tablespoons fresh lemon juice
1½   tablespoons water
1   tablespoon low-sodium Worcestershire sauce
2   teaspoons olive oil
¼   teaspoon garlic powder
6   anchovies, cut in half crosswise
     Dash of freshly ground pepper

Per Serving:
Carbohydrate 13.4g
Protein 5.2g
Fat 4.4g
Fiber 1.3g
Cholesterol 3mg
Sodium 347mg
Calcium 80mg
Exchanges
1 Vegetable
½ Grain
½ Lean Meat
½ Fat

1 Cut bread into ½-inch cubes; place cubes on a baking sheet. Coat cubes on all sides with cooking spray; sprinkle with ½ teaspoon garlic powder. Broil 3 inches from heat (with electric oven door partially opened) until toasted on all sides, turning frequently.

2 Combine lettuce and cheese in a large bowl. Combine lemon juice and next 4 ingredients, stirring with a wire whisk until blended. Pour over lettuce mixture; toss gently to coat.

3 Arrange lettuce mixture on salad plates, and top with anchovy halves. Sprinkle with bread cubes and freshly ground pepper. Serve immediately.

Yield: 4 servings (114 calories per serving).

Couscous and Cucumber Salad

Couscous and Cucumber Salad

Time: Prep 20 minutes; Chill 20 minutes

Per Serving:		
Carbohydrate 29.3g	¼	cup sugar
Protein 5.5g	¼	cup white wine vinegar
Fat 0.2g	¼	teaspoon salt
Fiber 1.3g	1	cup seeded, diced cucumber
Cholesterol 0mg	1	cup water
Sodium 138mg	1	cup couscous, uncooked
Calcium 62mg	1	teaspoon dried dillweed
Exchanges	40	Belgian endive leaves (about 4 heads)
1½ Grain	16	tomato slices (¼ inch thick)
1 Vegetable		Yogurt Dressing
		Fresh dillweed sprigs (optional)

1 Combine first 3 ingredients; stir. Add cucumber, and toss. Cover and chill.

2 Bring water to a boil in a saucepan; remove from heat. Add couscous; cover and let stand 5 minutes or until couscous is tender and liquid is absorbed.

3 Fluff couscous with a fork, and transfer to a medium bowl. Stir in cucumber mixture and dried dillweed. Cover and chill thoroughly.

4 Place 5 endive leaves and 2 tomato slices on each individual salad plate. Spoon couscous mixture over tomato and endive. Drizzle Yogurt Dressing over each salad. Garnish with dillweed sprigs, if desired.

Yield: 8 servings (142 calories per serving).

Yogurt Dressing

½   cup plain nonfat yogurt
½   cup nonfat sour cream
¼   teaspoon dried dillweed
⅛   teaspoon salt

1 Combine all ingredients, stirring well. Yield: 1 cup.

Orzo Salad

Time: Prep 10 minutes; Chill 2 hours

1   cup orzo, uncooked
1   (7-ounce) jar sun-dried tomatoes in olive oil
½   cup chopped sweet red pepper
¼   cup chopped green onions
3   tablespoons chopped fresh parsley
1   (4-ounce) can sliced ripe olives, drained
¼   cup red wine vinegar
¼   teaspoon dry mustard

Per Serving:
Carbohydrate 22.0g
Protein 3.9g
Fat 1.5g
Fiber 1.7g
Cholesterol 0mg
Sodium 154mg
Calcium 19mg
Exchanges
1½ Grain

1 Cook orzo according to package directions, omitting salt and fat; drain.

2 Drain tomatoes, reserving 1 teaspoon oil. Chop 2 tablespoons tomato. Reserve remaining tomatoes for another use. Combine orzo, tomato, red pepper, and next 3 ingredients in a bowl; toss gently.

3 Combine reserved 1 teaspoon oil, vinegar, and mustard; stir well with a wire whisk. Pour over orzo mixture; toss gently. Cover and chill at least 2 hours.

Yield: 8 (½-cup) servings (116 calories per serving).

Warm Black Bean and Spinach Salad

Time: Prep 16 minutes; Cook 11 minutes

Per Serving:
Carbohydrate 27.9g
Protein 10.3g
Fat 3.1g
Fiber 5.3g
Cholesterol 0mg
Sodium 333mg
Calcium 85mg
Exchanges
1 Vegetable
1½ Grain
1 Lean Meat

1 tablespoon vegetable oil
1 cup chopped onion
¼ cup sliced green onions
1 clove garlic, crushed
½ cup chopped sweet red pepper
1 (15-ounce) can black beans, drained
2 tablespoons water
2 tablespoons white wine vinegar
2 tablespoons balsamic vinegar
⅛ teaspoon salt
⅛ teaspoon crushed red pepper
⅛ teaspoon black pepper
4 cups tightly packed prepackaged fresh spinach

1 Heat oil in a large nonstick skillet over medium heat. Add onion, green onions, and garlic; sauté 4 minutes. Add chopped pepper; sauté 2 minutes. Add beans and remaining ingredients; cook 2 minutes or until thoroughly heated, stirring frequently. Place spinach in a large bowl; pour bean mixture over spinach; toss.

Yield: 6 (1-cup) servings (173 calories per serving).

Southwestern Crabmeat Salad

Time: Prep 17 minutes

Per Serving:
Carbohydrate 13.9g
Protein 13.8g
Fat 2.1g
Fiber 2.1g
Cholesterol 57mg
Sodium 255mg
Calcium 116mg
Exchanges
1 Grain
1½ Lean Meat

6 (6-inch) corn tortillas
¾ pound fresh lump crabmeat, drained
½ cup chopped tomato
½ cup chopped green pepper
¼ cup chopped onion
2 tablespoons chopped fresh cilantro
2 tablespoons lime juice
1 tablespoon white wine vinegar
1 teaspoon minced jalapeño pepper
⅛ teaspoon salt
1 small clove garlic, minced
1½ cups shredded curly leaf lettuce

1 Place tortillas on a large baking sheet. Bake at 350° for 15 minutes or until crisp. Set aside.

2 Combine crabmeat and next 4 ingredients in a bowl. Combine lime juice and next 4 ingredients. Add to crabmeat mixture, stirring well.

3 Place tortillas on individual salad plates. Top each with ¼ cup lettuce and ½ cup crabmeat mixture.

Yield: 6 servings (128 calories per serving).

Southwestern Crabmeat Salad

Spicy Tuna-Pasta Toss

Time: Prep 12 minutes; Chill 15 minutes

Per Serving:
Carbohydrate 24.8g
Protein 16.9g
Fat 7.2g
Fiber 0.9g
Cholesterol 26mg
Sodium 341mg
Calcium 9mg
Exchanges
2 Vegetable
1 Grain
2 Lean Meat

6   ounces tri-colored corkscrew pasta, uncooked
2   (6⅛-ounce) cans chunk white tuna in spring water, drained
½   cup sweet yellow pepper strips
½   quartered cherry tomatoes
¼   cup diced celery
¾   cup no-salt-added salsa
½   cup reduced-calorie mayonnaise
½   teaspoon ground red pepper
    Curly leaf lettuce leaves (optional)
2   tablespoons sliced green onions

1 Cook pasta according to package directions, omitting salt and fat. Drain; rinse under cold water, and drain. Combine pasta, tuna, and next 3 ingredients.

2 Combine salsa, mayonnaise, and red pepper. Add to pasta mixture; toss. Cover and chill. Serve in a lettuce-lined bowl, if desired; sprinkle with onions.

Yield: 6 (1-cup) servings (236 calories per serving).

"When I eat out I always ask for my salad with the dressing on the side. Then I dip my fork into the dressing, avoiding unnecessary fat and calories. Try it. Make it a habit."— Jenny

Buttermilk-Herb Dressing

Time: Prep 5 minutes; Chill at least 20 minutes

1	cup nonfat buttermilk
⅓	cup low-fat sour cream
3	tablespoons reduced-calorie mayonnaise
1	tablespoon grated Parmesan cheese
¾	teaspoon freeze-dried chives
¼	teaspoon garlic powder
⅛	teaspoon salt
⅛	teaspoon pepper

Per Tablespoon:
Carbohydrate 0.8g
Protein 0.6g
Fat 1.0g
Fiber 0g
Cholesterol 2mg
Sodium 42mg
Calcium 19mg
Exchange
Free

1 Combine all ingredients in a bowl; stir well with a wire whisk. Cover and chill. Serve with salad greens.

Yield: 1½ cups (14 calories per tablespoon).

Orange Curry Dressing

Time: Prep 5 minutes; Chill at least 10 minutes

1	(8-ounce) carton plain nonfat yogurt
¼	cup low-sugar orange marmalade
1	teaspoon lemon juice
½	teaspoon curry powder
¼	teaspoon ground ginger

Per Tablespoon:
Carbohydrate 1.2g
Protein 0.8g
Fat 0.0g
Fiber 0g
Cholesterol 0mg
Sodium 10mg
Calcium 27mg
Exchange
Free

1 Combine all ingredients in a bowl, stirring well. Cover and chill thoroughly. Serve with fresh fruit.

Yield: 1 cup plus 2 tablespoons (8 calories per tablespoon).

Dijon-Herb Vinaigrette

Time: Prep 5 minutes; Chill at least 20 minutes

Per Tablespoon:
Carbohydrate 0.6g
Protein 0.1g
Fat 0.8g
Fiber 0g
Cholesterol 0mg
Sodium 38mg
Calcium 3mg
Exchange
Free

⅓ cup white wine vinegar
¼ cup plus 1 tablespoon water
2 tablespoons chopped fresh chives
1½ tablespoons minced shallots
1 tablespoon minced fresh dillweed
1 tablespoon Dijon mustard
1 teaspoon minced fresh oregano
1 teaspoon minced fresh thyme
2 teaspoons olive oil
¼ teaspoon sugar

1 Combine all ingredients in a small jar; cover tightly, and shake vigorously to blend. Chill thoroughly. Serve with salad greens.

Yield: ¾ cup (11 calories per tablespoon).

Raspberry Vinaigrette

Time: Prep 5 minutes; Chill at least 20 minutes

Per Tablespoon:
Carbohydrate 0.9g
Protein 0.1g
Fat 0.8g
Fiber 0g
Cholesterol 0mg
Sodium 0mg
Calcium 2mg
Exchange
Free

¼ cup unsweetened orange juice
1½ tablespoons minced fresh chives
2 tablespoons plus 1 teaspoon water
2 tablespoons red wine vinegar
2 tablespoons raspberry vinegar
2 teaspoons olive oil
½ teaspoon dried dillweed
¼ teaspoon pepper

1 Combine all ingredients in a small jar; cover tightly, and shake vigorously to blend. Chill. Serve with salad greens.

Yield: ¾ cup (10 calories per tablespoon).

Side Dishes

Siesta Pasta (page 189)

Herbed Bulgur Pilaf

Time: Prep 5 minutes; Cook 12 minutes

Per Serving:
Carbohydrate 21.7g
Protein 3.1g
Fat 2.6g
Fiber 1.5g
Cholesterol 0mg
Sodium 113mg
Calcium 69mg
Exchanges
1½ Grain

Vegetable cooking spray
2 teaspoons vegetable oil
½ cup coarsely shredded carrot
¼ cup thinly sliced green onions
1 large clove garlic, minced
1 cup hot water
½ cup bulgur wheat, uncooked
2 teaspoons honey
½ teaspoon chicken-flavored bouillon granules
½ teaspoon dried mint flakes
½ teaspoon dried basil

1 Coat a large nonstick skillet with cooking spray; add oil. Place over medium-high heat until hot. Add carrot, green onions, and garlic; sauté 1 minute.

2 Add water and remaining ingredients; stir well. Bring to a boil; cover, reduce heat, and simmer 12 to 15 minutes or until bulgur is tender and liquid is absorbed. Fluff bulgur with a fork, and transfer to a serving bowl.

Yield: 4 (½-cup) servings (122 calories per serving).

Oriental Couscous

Time: Prep 5 minutes; Cook 5 minutes

Per Serving:
Carbohydrate 26.9g
Protein 4.5g
Fat 0.1g
Fiber 0.7g
Cholesterol 0mg
Sodium 132mg
Calcium 19mg
Exchanges
1½ Grain

Vegetable cooking spray
½ cup sliced green onions
1½ cups water
2 tablespoons low-sodium soy sauce
½ teaspoon sugar
¼ teaspoon ground ginger
¼ teaspoon garlic powder
¼ teaspoon ground red pepper
1 cup couscous, uncooked

1 Coat a medium saucepan with cooking spray; place over medium-high heat until hot. Add green onions, and sauté until tender.

2 Add water and next 5 ingredients; bring to a boil. Remove from heat. Add couscous; cover and let stand 5 minutes or until couscous is tender and liquid is absorbed. Fluff couscous with a fork, and transfer to a serving bowl.

Yield: 6 (½-cup) servings (131 calories per serving).

Four Grain Pilaf

Time: Prep 10 minutes; Cook 30 minutes

1	tablespoon reduced-calorie margarine
½	cup chopped shallots
¼	cup quinoa, uncooked
1	cup long-grain rice, uncooked
½	cup bulgur wheat, uncooked
¼	cup barley, uncooked
3	cups canned no-salt-added beef broth, undiluted
½	teaspoon salt
½	teaspoon pepper
¼	cup chopped fresh parsley

Per Serving:
Carbohydrate 29.3g
Protein 3.8g
Fat 1.2g
Fiber 1.7g
Cholesterol 0mg
Sodium 134mg
Calcium 14mg
Exchanges
2 Grain

1 Heat margarine in a large saucepan over medium-high heat until margarine melts. Add shallots, and sauté 2 to 3 minutes or until tender.

2 Rinse quinoa in 3 changes of water; drain. Add quinoa, rice, bulgur, and barley to saucepan; stir well. Cook 5 minutes, stirring constantly. Add beef broth, salt, and pepper. Bring to a boil; cover, reduce heat, and simmer 25 minutes or until grains are tender and broth is absorbed. Fluff with a fork, and stir in parsley. Serve immediately.

Yield: 10 (½-cup) servings (147 calories per serving).

"Try cooking rice and other grains in chicken, beef or vegetable broth—you'll enjoy the flavor that permeates each individual grain." —Jenny

Fragrant Basmati Rice

Time: Prep 3 minutes; Cook 20 minutes

Per Serving:
Carbohydrate 25.6g
Protein 2.3g
Fat 0.2g
Fiber 0.4g
Cholesterol 0mg
Sodium 148mg
Calcium 11mg
Exchanges
1½ Grain

1¼ cups basmati rice
2½ cups water
½ teaspoon salt
¼ teaspoon ground cardamom
¼ teaspoon ground turmeric
¼ teaspoon ground red pepper
⅛ teaspoon ground cinnamon
Dash of saffron

1 Combine all ingredients in a medium saucepan. Bring to a boil, and stir. Cover, reduce heat, and simmer 20 minutes.

2 Remove from heat, and let stand 5 minutes.

Yield: 8 (½-cup) servings (117 calories per serving).

Hint-of-Spice Rice

Time: Prep 5 minutes; Cook 30 minutes

Per Serving:
Carbohydrate 24.6g
Protein 3.9g
Fat 3.5g
Fiber 2.0g
Cholesterol 0mg
Sodium 143mg
Calcium 25mg
Exchanges
1½ Grain
1 Fat

1½ cups canned low-sodium chicken broth, undiluted
¾ cup long-grain brown rice, uncooked
1 teaspoon grated orange rind
¼ teaspoon salt
¼ teaspoon ground ginger
¼ teaspoon ground cinnamon
1 medium orange, peeled and sectioned
¼ cup sliced almonds, toasted

1 Combine first 6 ingredients in a large saucepan; bring to a boil. Cover, reduce heat, and simmer 30 minutes or until rice is tender and liquid is absorbed.

2 Gently stir in orange sections and almonds.

Yield: 5 (½-cup) servings (143 calories per serving).

Easy Spanish Rice

Time: Prep 10 minutes; Cook 25 minutes

Vegetable cooking spray
- ½ cup chopped green pepper
- ½ cup chopped onion
- 2 (8-ounce) cans no-salt-added tomato sauce
- 1 (14½-ounce) can no-salt-added stewed tomatoes, undrained and chopped
- 1 cup long-grain rice, uncooked
- ¼ cup water
- 1 teaspoon chili powder
- ½ teaspoon dried oregano
- ¼ teaspoon salt
- ¼ teaspoon ground red pepper
- ¼ teaspoon ground cumin

Per Serving:
Carbohydrate 27.7g
Protein 3.0g
Fat 0.3g
Fiber 0.7g
Cholesterol 0mg
Sodium 99mg
Calcium 27mg
Exchanges
1 Vegetable
1½ Grain

1 Coat a nonstick skillet with cooking spray; place over medium-high heat until hot. Add green pepper and onion; sauté 5 minutes or until tender.

2 Add tomato sauce and remaining ingredients. Bring to a boil; cover, reduce heat, and simmer 25 minutes or until rice is tender and liquid is absorbed.

Yield: 8 (½-cup) servings (125 calories per serving).

Easy Spanish Rice

Mediterranean Linguine

Mediterranean Linguine

Time: Prep 15 minutes; Cook 10 minutes

Per Serving:		
		Vegetable cooking spray
Carbohydrate 16.9g	1	cup sliced fresh mushrooms
Protein 4.4g	1	medium-size green pepper, seeded and cut into thin strips
Fat 1.6g	1	medium-size sweet red pepper, seeded and cut into thin strips
Fiber 2.5g	1	clove garlic, minced
Cholesterol 3mg	1	(14-ounce) can artichoke hearts, drained and quartered
Sodium 192mg	½	cup commercial oil-free Italian dressing
Calcium 55mg	3	tablespoons sliced, pitted ripe olives
Exchanges	1	tablespoon chopped fresh parsley
1 Grain	6	ounces linguine, uncooked
1 Fat	½	cup (2 ounces) shredded part-skim mozzarella cheese

1 Coat a large nonstick skillet with cooking spray; place over medium-high heat until hot. Add mushrooms and next 3 ingredients; sauté until vegetables are crisp-tender. Add artichokes, Italian dressing, olives, and parsley; cook 3 minutes or until thoroughly heated, stirring occasionally.

2 Cook linguine according to package directions, omitting salt and fat; drain well.

3 Combine linguine and vegetable mixture; toss well. Transfer mixture to a serving dish; sprinkle with cheese, and serve immediately.

Yield: 11 (½-cup) servings (94 calories per serving).

Linguine Florentine

Time: Prep 15 minutes; Cook 15 minutes

2	pounds fresh spinach
3	cups cooked linguine (cooked without salt or fat)
2	teaspoons olive oil
½	cup grated Parmesan cheese
¼	teaspoon pepper
1	tablespoon chopped walnuts, toasted

Per Serving:
Carbohydrate 25.7g
Protein 9.1g
Fat 5.7g
Fiber 2.6g
Cholesterol 7mg
Sodium 199mg
Calcium 165mg
Exchanges
2 Vegetable
1 Grain
1 Fat

1 Remove and discard stems from spinach; wash leaves thoroughly. Place spinach in a large Dutch oven (do not add water); cover and cook over medium heat about 4 minutes or until wilted.

2 Drain spinach well, and squeeze between paper towels until barely moist. Finely chop spinach, and set aside.

3 Combine linguine and oil in a large bowl, tossing gently. Add spinach, cheese, and pepper; toss gently. Transfer to a serving bowl; sprinkle with walnuts.

Yield: 6 (1-cup) servings (191 calories per serving).

Easy Noodle Bake

Time: Prep 15 minutes; Cook 25 minutes

Per Serving:
Carbohydrate 19.8g
Protein 6.0g
Fat 1.3g
Fiber 0.3g
Cholesterol 23mg
Sodium 152mg
Calcium 18mg
Exchanges
1 Vegetable
1 Grain

Vegetable cooking spray
¾ cup sliced fresh mushrooms
1 clove garlic, minced
2½ cups cooked medium noodles (cooked without salt or fat)
¾ cup nonfat sour cream
2 tablespoons chopped green onions
2 tablespoons chopped fresh parsley
1 tablespoon diced pimiento
¼ teaspoon salt
¼ teaspoon pepper
1 tablespoon grated Parmesan cheese

1 Coat a large nonstick skillet with cooking spray; place over medium-high heat until hot. Add mushrooms and garlic; sauté until mushrooms are tender. Remove from heat; add noodles and next 6 ingredients, stirring gently.

2 Transfer mixture to a 1-quart casserole coated with cooking spray; top with cheese. Cover and bake at 350° for 20 minutes or until thoroughly heated; uncover and bake 5 minutes or until cheese is browned.

Yield: 6 (½-cup) servings (118 calories per serving).

Tortellini with Zucchini and Tomatoes

Time: Prep 22 minutes; Cook 5 minutes

Per Serving:
Carbohydrate 47.7g
Protein 12.1g
Fat 6.9g
Fiber 0.4g
Cholesterol 30mg
Sodium 384mg
Calcium 167mg
Exchanges
1 Vegetable
3 Grain
1 Fat

¼ cup sun-dried tomatoes
½ cup hot water
Olive oil-flavored vegetable cooking spray
1 tablespoon olive oil
1 cup chopped zucchini
3 cloves garlic, minced
2 green onions, cut into 1-inch pieces
¼ cup chopped sweet red pepper
1 teaspoon dried oregano
1 (9-ounce) package fresh cheese tortellini

1 Combine tomatoes and water in a small bowl; cover and let stand 15 minutes. Drain tomatoes, and slice thinly; set aside.

2 Coat a large nonstick skillet with cooking spray; add oil. Place over medium-high heat until hot. Add zucchini and garlic; sauté 2 minutes. Add green onions, red pepper, and oregano; sauté 1 minute. Stir in tomato. Remove from heat, and keep warm.

3 Cook tortellini according to package directions, omitting salt and fat; drain. Place tortellini in a bowl. Add zucchini mixture; toss. Serve immediately.

Yield: 4 (1-cup) servings (249 calories per serving).

Siesta Pasta

Time: Prep 10 minutes; Cook 20 minutes

		Per Serving:
6	ounces spaghetti, uncooked	*Carbohydrate 22.0g*
	Vegetable cooking spray	*Protein 5.3g*
1	cup fresh broccoli flowerets	*Fat 1.8g*
1	cup thinly sliced carrot	*Fiber 2.2g*
1	cup sliced zucchini	*Cholesterol 3mg*
¼	cup sliced onion	*Sodium 119mg*
1	small sweet yellow pepper, seeded and cut into julienne strips	*Calcium 67mg*
⅓	cup chopped green pepper	Exchanges
10	cherry tomatoes, halved	1½ Grain
2	tablespoons commercial oil-free Italian dressing	
¼	cup grated Parmesan cheese	
1	tablespoon minced fresh parsley	
¼	teaspoon sweet red pepper flakes	

1 Cook spaghetti according to package directions, omitting salt and fat. Drain; set aside.

2 Coat a nonstick skillet with cooking spray; place over medium-high heat until hot. Add broccoli and next 3 ingredients; sauté 4 minutes. Add peppers; sauté 4 minutes. Add spaghetti, tomatoes, and Italian dressing; cook until heated.

3 Transfer to a serving bowl. Sprinkle with cheese, parsley, and pepper flakes; toss gently to combine. Serve immediately.

Yield: 8 (1-cup) servings (123 calories per serving).

Vermicelli with Tomato-Basil Sauce

Time: Prep 10 minutes; Cook 30 minutes

Per Serving:
Carbohydrate 30.8g
Protein 5.8g
Fat 1.4g
Fiber 2.5g
Cholesterol 1mg
Sodium 47mg
Calcium 46mg
Exchanges
2 Grain

8	ounces vermicelli, uncooked
	Vegetable cooking spray
1	medium onion, thinly sliced
2	cloves garlic, minced
5	cups peeled, chopped tomato (about 5 medium)
1	(8-ounce) can no-salt-added tomato sauce
¼	cup minced fresh basil
⅛	teaspoon pepper
2	tablespoons grated Parmesan cheese

1 Cook vermicelli according to package directions, omitting salt and fat. Drain well, and set aside.

2 Coat a Dutch oven with cooking spray; place over medium heat until hot. Add onion and minced garlic; sauté 5 minutes or until onion is tender. Stir in tomato, tomato sauce, basil, and pepper. Bring to a boil; reduce heat, and simmer 15 minutes, stirring occasionally.

3 Add vermicelli; cook, uncovered, until thoroughly heated, stirring occasionally. Transfer mixture to a large platter; sprinkle with Parmesan cheese.

Yield: 8 (1-cup) servings (155 calories per serving).

"The most time-consuming part of cooking pasta is waiting for the water to boil. To hasten the process, I put the water on to boil as soon as I enter the kitchen. I cover the pot with a lid, too; this traps in the heat so the water boils faster." — Jenny

Asparagus Dijon

Asparagus Dijon

Time: Prep 10 minutes; Cook 10 minutes

1½ pounds fresh asparagus spears
1 cup nonfat buttermilk
1 tablespoon cornstarch
2 teaspoons Dijon mustard
¾ teaspoon lemon juice
½ teaspoon dried tarragon
¼ teaspoon ground white pepper

1 Snap off tough ends of asparagus. Remove scales from spears with a knife or vegetable peeler, if desired. Arrange asparagus in a vegetable steamer over boiling water. Cover and steam 7 minutes or until crisp-tender. Set aside, and keep warm.

2 Combine buttermilk and cornstarch in a saucepan; stir well. Cook over medium heat, stirring constantly, until thickened and bubbly. Remove from heat; stir in mustard and remaining ingredients. Spoon over asparagus. Serve immediately.

Yield: 6 servings (42 calories per serving).

Per Serving:
Carbohydrate 6.5g
Protein 4.1g
Fat 0.5g
Fiber 1.8g
Cholesterol 0mg
Sodium 94mg
Calcium 11mg
Exchange
1 Vegetable

Spicy Black Beans and Tomatoes

Time: Prep 5 minutes; Cook 13 minutes

Per Serving:
Carbohydrate 18.8g
Protein 6.1g
Fat 1.1g
Fiber 2.8g
Cholesterol 0mg
Sodium 187mg
Calcium 44mg
Exchanges
1 Vegetable
1 Grain

Vegetable cooking spray
1   teaspoon olive oil
½   cup chopped onion
2   cloves garlic, minced
2   (14½-ounce) cans no-salt-added whole tomatoes, drained and chopped
2   tablespoons canned chopped green chiles
2   (15-ounce) cans black beans, rinsed and drained
1   tablespoon chopped fresh cilantro
½   teaspoon ground cumin
½   teaspoon ground red pepper
¼   teaspoon chili powder

1 Coat a large nonstick skillet with cooking spray; add oil. Place over medium-high heat until hot. Add onion and garlic; sauté until tender. Add tomato and chiles; reduce heat, and cook, uncovered, 6 to 8 minutes or until mixture is slightly thickened, stirring occasionally.

2 Stir in beans and remaining ingredients. Cover and cook 5 minutes or until thoroughly heated.

Yield: 8 (½-cup) servings (104 calories per serving).

Italian Broccoli and Tomatoes

Time: Prep 5 minutes; Cook 15 minutes

Per Serving:
Carbohydrate 4.9g
Protein 3.8g
Fat 0.9g
Fiber 1.9g
Cholesterol 1mg
Sodium 111mg
Calcium 76mg
Exchange
1 Vegetable

1   pound fresh broccoli
2   medium tomatoes, cut into 8 wedges
2   tablespoons water
½   teaspoon garlic powder
½   teaspoon dried oregano
½   cup (2 ounces) shredded nonfat mozzarella cheese
2   tablespoons sliced ripe olives

1 Trim off large leaves of broccoli, and remove tough ends of lower stalks. Wash broccoli thoroughly, and cut into small spears. Arrange broccoli in a vegetable steamer over boiling water. Cover and steam 5 to 8 minutes or until crisp-tender. Drain.

2 Place broccoli in a saucepan. Add tomato, water, garlic powder, and oregano; stir gently. Cook, uncovered, over medium-low heat 10 to 15 minutes or until thoroughly heated, stirring occasionally. Sprinkle with cheese and olives.

3 Remove from heat. Cover and let stand 2 to 3 minutes or until cheese melts.

Yield: 8 (½-cup) servings (37 calories per serving).

Italian Broccoli and Tomatoes

Ginger-Mint Carrots

Time: Prep 5 minutes; Cook 9 minutes

Per Serving:
Carbohydrate 10.8g
Protein 0.8g
Fat 0.1g
Fiber 2.5g
Cholesterol 0mg
Sodium 29mg
Calcium 24mg
Exchanges
2 Vegetable

4½ cups diagonally sliced carrot (about 1½ pounds)
1 tablespoon minced crystallized ginger
1 tablespoon mint jelly
1 teaspoon minced fresh mint

1 Arrange carrot in a vegetable steamer over boiling water. Cover and steam 8 minutes or until crisp-tender. Transfer to a serving bowl; keep warm.

2 Combine ginger, jelly, and mint in a small saucepan, stirring well. Cook over medium heat 1 minute or until jelly melts. Pour over carrot; toss well.

Yield: 7 (½-cup) servings (45 calories per serving).

Creamy Cauliflower-Pea Medley

Time: Prep 4 minutes; Cook 5 minutes

Per Serving:
Carbohydrate 15.7g
Protein 6.0g
Fat 2.4g
Fiber 5.1g
Cholesterol 3mg
Sodium 213mg
Calcium 47mg
Exchanges
3 Vegetable

½ cup water
1 (10-ounce) package frozen cauliflower
1 (10-ounce) package frozen English peas
1 cup peeled, diced cucumber
3 tablespoons commercial reduced-calorie ranch dressing
2 tablespoons nonfat sour cream
¼ teaspoon dried dillweed

1 Combine first 3 ingredients in a saucepan; bring to a boil. Cover and cook 5 minutes; drain well.

2 Combine cauliflower mixture and remaining ingredients in a bowl; toss well. Serve warm or chilled.

Yield: 4 (1-cup) servings (104 calories per serving).

Basil-Lemon Snap Peas

Time: Prep 5 minutes; Cook 5 minutes

2	teaspoons olive oil
1	clove garlic, minced
1½	pounds Sugar Snap peas, trimmed
1	cup chopped sweet yellow pepper
⅓	cup chopped fresh basil
½	teaspoon sugar
½	teaspoon grated lemon rind
¼	teaspoon salt
¼	teaspoon pepper
2	tablespoons fresh lemon juice

Per Serving:
Carbohydrate 9.8g
Protein 3.0g
Fat 1.8g
Fiber 3.0g
Cholesterol 0mg
Sodium 103mg
Calcium 53mg
Exchanges
2 Vegetable

1 Heat oil in a large nonstick skillet over medium-high heat until hot. Add garlic, and sauté 30 seconds. Add peas and yellow pepper; sauté 2 to 3 minutes or until peas are crisp-tender. Add basil and next 4 ingredients; sauté 30 seconds. Add lemon juice, and sauté 30 seconds. Serve immediately.

Yield: 6 (1-cup) servings (65 calories per serving).

Grilled Pepper and Squash

Time: Prep 5 minutes; Cook 5 minutes

1	large sweet red pepper, seeded and cut into wide strips
2	small yellow squash, cut into ¼-inch-thick slices
1	medium zucchini, cut into ¼-inch-thick slices
1	purple onion, cut into wedges
2	teaspoons fresh rosemary
	Vegetable cooking spray

Per Serving:
Carbohydrate 8.3g
Protein 1.5g
Fat 0.3g
Fiber 2.1g
Cholesterol 0mg
Sodium 4mg
Calcium 25mg
Exchange
1 Vegetable

1 Combine first 5 ingredients in a large bowl, tossing gently to combine.

2 Coat grill basket with cooking spray. Place vegetable mixture in basket. Grill over medium-hot coals (350° to 400°) 5 minutes; turn basket, and grill 5 additional minutes.

Yield: 4 servings (37 calories per serving).

Mushroom and Leek Sauté

Time: Prep 10 minutes; Cook 10 minutes

Per Serving:
Carbohydrate 7.1g
Protein 1.8g
Fat 1.7g
Fiber 1.2g
Cholesterol 0mg
Sodium 141mg
Calcium 22mg
Exchange
1 Vegetable

1   tablespoon plus 1 teaspoon reduced-calorie margarine
2   cups sliced leeks
1   pound fresh mushrooms, quartered
2   tablespoons low-sodium soy sauce
½   teaspoon dried oregano
¼   teaspoon pepper

1 Melt margarine in a nonstick skillet over medium-high heat. Add leeks; sauté 3 minutes. Add mushrooms and remaining ingredients; sauté 4 minutes or until mushrooms are tender.

Yield: 7 (½-cup) servings (47 calories per serving).

Creamy Sliced Potatoes

Time: Prep 10 minutes; Cook 20 minutes

Per Serving:
Carbohydrate 17.4g
Protein 3.0g
Fat 1.1g
Fiber 1.1g
Cholesterol 1mg
Sodium 111mg
Calcium 43mg
Exchange
1 Grain

1¼   pounds round red potatoes, cut into ¼-inch-thick slices
1   tablespoon reduced-calorie margarine
1½   tablespoons all-purpose flour
1   cup skim milk
¼   teaspoon salt
¼   teaspoon dried dillweed
⅛   teaspoon pepper
¼   cup nonfat sour cream

1 Cook potato in a large saucepan in boiling water to cover 10 to 15 minutes or until tender. Drain. Place in a medium bowl; set aside, and keep warm.

2 Melt margarine in a small saucepan over low heat; add flour, stirring until smooth. Cook 1 minute, stirring constantly with a wire whisk. Gradually add milk; cook over medium heat, stirring constantly, until mixture is thickened and bubbly. Stir in salt, dillweed, and pepper. Remove from heat, and stir in sour cream. Add to potato; toss gently. Serve warm.

Yield: 8 (½-cup) servings (90 calories per serving).

Curried Sweet Potato Strips

Time: Prep 10 minutes; Cook 45 minutes

3	small sweet potatoes, peeled (about 1½ pounds)
1	tablespoon plus 1 teaspoon vegetable oil
1	tablespoon unsweetened apple juice
½	teaspoon curry powder
	Vegetable cooking spray

1 Cut each potato lengthwise into 14 thin wedges; place in a large heavy-duty, zip-top plastic bag. Add oil, apple juice, and curry powder to bag. Seal bag, and shake until potato wedges are well coated.

2 Remove wedges from bag, and place in a single layer on a 15- x 10- x 1-inch jellyroll pan coated with cooking spray. Bake at 400° for 45 minutes or until crisp and lightly browned, stirring every 10 minutes. Serve immediately.

Yield: 4 servings (189 calories per serving).

Per Serving:

Carbohydrate 34.2g
Protein 2.3g
Fat 5.2g
Fiber 4.2g
Cholesterol 0mg
Sodium 18mg
Calcium 32mg
Exchanges
2 Grain
1 Fat

Color Your World

It's no fluke of nature that carrots are orange and tomatoes are red. Carotenoids that give fruits and vegetables their brilliant colors have potential health benefits. As an antioxidant, it helps prevent damage to body cells by free radicals, possibly preventing some types of cancer and heart disease. Orange-yellow beta carotene is found in carrots, sweet potatoes, apricots, and leafy green vegetables.

Lemon Squash

Time: Prep 5 minutes; Cook 10 minutes

Per Serving:
Carbohydrate 5.8g
Protein 1.4g
Fat 1.4g
Fiber 1.4g
Cholesterol 0mg
Sodium 168mg
Calcium 26mg
Exchange
1 Vegetable

2¼ cups diagonally sliced yellow squash
2¼ cups diagonally sliced zucchini
¼ cup canned no-salt-added chicken broth, undiluted
1 tablespoon lemon juice
1 teaspoon cornstarch
2 teaspoons reduced-calorie margarine
¼ teaspoon dried oregano
¼ teaspoon salt
¼ teaspoon pepper

1 Arrange squash and zucchini in a vegetable steamer over boiling water. Cover and steam 6 minutes or until crisp-tender; place in a serving bowl.

2 Combine chicken broth and remaining ingredients in a small saucepan, stirring until smooth. Cook over medium heat, stirring constantly, until slightly thickened. Pour mixture over vegetables; toss gently.

Yield: 4 (1-cup) servings (36 calories per serving).

Vegetable-Stuffed Zucchini

Time: Prep 18 minutes; Cook 20 minutes

Per Serving:
Carbohydrate 4.3g
Protein 2.6g
Fat 1.1g
Fiber 0.9g
Cholesterol 3mg
Sodium 112mg
Calcium 53mg
Exchange
1 Vegetable

4 medium zucchini (about 1½ pounds)
¾ cup finely chopped tomato
⅓ cup chopped green pepper
¼ cup chopped onion
¼ teaspoon salt
¼ teaspoon dried basil
¼ teaspoon dried oregano
⅓ cup (1.3 ounces) shredded reduced-fat Cheddar cheese

1 Place zucchini in a large saucepan with water to cover. Bring to a boil; cover, reduce heat, and simmer 4 to 6 minutes or until crisp-tender. Drain and let cool.

2 Cut zucchini in half lengthwise. Scoop out pulp, leaving ¼-inch-thick shells. Chop pulp; reserve shells.

Vegetable-Stuffed Zucchini

3 Combine zucchini pulp, tomato, and next 5 ingredients; stir well. Spoon into zucchini shells. Place shells in a 13- x 9- x 2-inch baking dish. Bake, uncovered, at 400° for 15 minutes. Sprinkle with cheese. Bake 5 additional minutes or until cheese melts.

Yield: 8 servings (34 calories per serving).

Sautéed Apple Rings with Orange Juice

Time: Prep 5 minutes; Cook 11 minutes

Per Serving:
Carbohydrate 16.9g
Protein 0.3g
Fat 0.9g
Fiber 2.4g
Cholesterol 0mg
Sodium 10mg
Calcium 14mg
Exchange
1 Fruit

2   small Winesap apples
¼   cup unsweetened orange juice
1   tablespoon brown sugar
1   teaspoon ground cinnamon
1   teaspoon reduced-calorie margarine

1 Core apples, and slice each crosswise into 6 rings.

2 Combine orange juice and remaining ingredients in a large nonstick skillet. Bring to a boil over medium heat, stirring until sugar dissolves.

3 Arrange apple rings in skillet in a single layer. Cook 5 to 6 minutes or until tender, turning once. Serve warm.

Yield: 4 servings (70 calories per serving).

Citrus Fruit Cocktail

Time: Prep 10 minutes

Per Serving:
Carbohydrate 19.9g
Protein 1.2g
Fat 0.3g
Fiber 3.3g
Cholesterol 0mg
Sodium 1mg
Calcium 31mg
Exchanges
1½ Fruit

2   medium oranges, peeled, sectioned, and coarsely chopped
1   medium-size pink grapefruit, peeled, sectioned, and coarsely chopped
2   kiwifruit, peeled and coarsely chopped
¼   teaspoon grated orange rind
¼   teaspoon grated lime rind
3   tablespoons unsweetened orange juice
1   tablespoon fresh lime juice
2   tablespoons honey

1 Combine first 3 ingredients in a medium bowl, and toss gently.

2 Combine orange rind and remaining ingredients in a small bowl; stir with a wire whisk until blended. Pour orange juice mixture over fruit, and toss gently.

Yield: 5 (½-cup) servings (81 calories per serving).

Soups & Sandwiches

Chicken-Crabmeat Pepperpot (page 206)

Cuban Black Bean Soup

Cuban Black Bean Soup

Time: Prep 10 minutes; Cook 50 minutes

Per Serving:
Carbohydrate 37.4g
Protein 14.8g
Fat 1.5g
Fiber 6.6g
Cholesterol 6mg
Sodium 192mg
Calcium 66mg
Exchanges
1 Vegetable
2 Grain
1 Lean Meat

3	(15-ounce) cans no-salt-added black beans, undrained
2	(13¾-ounce) cans low-sodium beef broth
1½	cups chopped onion
2	cups water
¾	cup chopped green pepper
2	teaspoons minced garlic
1	(14½-ounce) can no-salt-added whole tomatoes, undrained and chopped
1	(4½-ounce) can chopped green chiles, undrained
¼	pound extra-lean cooked ham, diced
½	cup red wine vinegar
1	teaspoon dried oregano
1	teaspoon dried thyme
1	teaspoon ground cumin
½	teaspoon coarsely ground pepper

1 Combine first 6 ingredients in a large Dutch oven; bring mixture to a boil. Cover, reduce heat, and simmer 20 minutes, stirring frequently.

2 Add tomato and remaining ingredients to bean mixture. Cook, uncovered, over low heat 30 additional minutes, stirring occasionally.

Yield: 10 (1½-cup) servings (220 calories per serving).

Summer Gazpacho

Time: Prep 10 minutes; Chill 8 hours

1	(10½-ounce) can low-sodium tomato soup, undiluted
1¾	cups no-salt-added tomato juice
⅔	cup peeled, seeded, and finely chopped cucumber
½	cup finely chopped green pepper
½	cup finely chopped tomato
⅓	cup finely chopped onion
2	tablespoons red wine vinegar
1	tablespoon commercial oil-free Italian dressing
1	tablespoon lemon juice
1	clove garlic, minced
½	teaspoon pepper
¼	teaspoon salt
¼	teaspoon hot sauce
	Thinly sliced cucumber (optional)

Per Serving:
Carbohydrate 14.7g
Protein 2.1g
Fat 1.4g
Fiber 1.5g
Cholesterol 0mg
Sodium 169mg
Calcium 22mg
Exchange
1 Vegetable

1 Combine tomato soup and next 12 ingredients in a large bowl; stir well. Cover and chill at least 8 hours.

2 To serve, ladle soup into individual bowls, and garnish with cucumber slices, if desired.

Yield: 5 (1-cup) servings (74 calories per serving).

Chicken-Crabmeat Pepperpot

Time: Prep 12 minutes; Cook 30 minutes

Per Serving:		
Carbohydrate 13.8g	5	(10½-ounce) cans low-sodium chicken broth
Protein 16.5g	1	cup chopped onion
Fat 3.0g	1	teaspoon minced garlic
Fiber 2.1g	2	cups shredded cooked chicken breast
Cholesterol 46mg	3	cups fresh corn cut from cob (about 5 ears)
Sodium 184mg	½	pound fresh lump crabmeat, drained
Calcium 34mg	1	medium-size sweet red pepper, cut into 1-inch pieces
Exchanges	1	medium-size green pepper, cut into 1-inch pieces
1 Vegetable	½	cup chopped green onions
½ Grain	½	cup chopped fresh cilantro
2 Lean Meat	1	teaspoon coarsely ground pepper
	¼	teaspoon salt

1 Combine first 3 ingredients in a large Dutch oven. Bring to a boil; cover, reduce heat, and simmer 10 minutes.

2 Add chicken and corn to broth. Bring to a boil; cover, reduce heat, and simmer 10 minutes. Stir in crabmeat and remaining ingredients; cover and cook 10 additional minutes or until vegetables are tender.

Yield: 11 (1-cup) servings.

"I've found that peppers—green, yellow, and red— will keep a week or two in the refrigerator if uncut. Roasted, peeled, and securely wrapped, they'll keep for months in the freezer. So stock up when pepper prices plunge!"—Jenny

Tortilla Soup

Time: Prep 5 minutes; Cook 30 minutes

2	(7-inch) flour tortillas
5	cups canned no-salt-added chicken broth, undiluted
1	cup chopped onion
2	teaspoons minced garlic
2	cups shredded cooked chicken breast
2	cups frozen corn with red and green peppers, thawed
¼	cup chopped green chiles, drained
¼	cup chopped ripe olives
½	teaspoon coarsely ground pepper
¼	teaspoon salt
¼	teaspoon ground cumin
¼	cup chopped fresh cilantro

Per Serving:
Carbohydrate 13.8g
Protein 15.4g
Fat 2.9g
Fiber 1.7g
Cholesterol 36mg
Sodium 218mg
Calcium 30mg
Exchanges
1 Grain
1½ Lean Meat

1 Cut tortillas into 2- x 1-inch strips. Set aside.

2 Bring broth, onion, and garlic to a boil in a large saucepan. Cover, reduce heat, and simmer 10 minutes. Add chicken and next 6 ingredients. Cook, uncovered, 15 minutes. Add tortilla strips and cilantro; cook 5 additional minutes.

Yield: 8 (1-cup) servings (149 calories per serving).

Cream of Carrot Soup

Time: Prep 35 minutes; Cook 30 minutes

Per Serving:
Carbohydrate 16.6g
Protein 2.9g
Fat 1.8g
Fiber 4.3g
Cholesterol 1mg
Sodium 173mg
Calcium 85mg
Exchanges
2 Vegetable
½ Grain

Vegetable cooking spray
1   tablespoon reduced-calorie margarine
2   pounds carrots, scraped and thinly sliced
1¼ cups chopped onion
1   cup sliced celery
3   cups canned low-sodium chicken broth, undiluted
1   cup 1% low-fat milk
¼   teaspoon salt
Fresh chives (optional)

1 Coat a Dutch oven with cooking spray; add margarine. Place over medium-high heat until margarine melts. Add carrot, onion, and celery; sauté 10 minutes. Add chicken broth; bring to a boil. Cover, reduce heat, and simmer 20 minutes. Remove from heat, and let cool 10 minutes.

2 Transfer mixture in batches to container of an electric blender or food processor; cover and process until smooth. Return puree to Dutch oven. Stir in milk and salt. Cook over medium heat just until thoroughly heated (do not boil). Ladle soup into individual bowls. Garnish with chives, if desired.

Yield: 7 (1-cup) servings (94 calories per serving).

Cream of Mushroom Soup

Time: Prep 15 minutes; Cook 10 minutes

Per Serving:
Carbohydrate 19.4g
Protein 10.5g
Fat 4.8g
Fiber 1.4g
Cholesterol 3mg
Sodium 423mg
Calcium 198mg
Exchanges
1 Vegetable
1 Skim Milk
1 Fat

Vegetable cooking spray
¾   pound sliced fresh mushrooms
¼   cup sliced green onions
2   tablespoons dry sherry
2   tablespoons reduced-calorie stick margarine
3   tablespoons all-purpose flour
2½ cups skim milk
1¼ teaspoons chicken-flavored bouillon granules
¼   teaspoon freshly ground pepper
⅔   cup nonfat sour cream
Green onion strips (optional)

1 Coat a large saucepan with cooking spray; place over medium-high heat until hot. Add mushrooms, ¼ cup green onions, and sherry; sauté until vegetables are tender. Set aside.

2 Melt margarine in a medium-size heavy saucepan over medium heat; add flour, stirring until smooth. Cook, stirring constantly, 1 minute. Gradually add milk; cook over medium heat, stirring constantly, 10 minutes or until mixture is thickened and bubbly.

3 Stir in mushroom mixture, bouillon granules, and pepper. Cook until thoroughly heated. Remove from heat, and stir in sour cream. Ladle soup into individual bowls. Garnish with onion strips, if desired.

Yield: 4 (1-cup) servings (161 calories per serving).

Cream of Mushroom Soup

Fish Chowder

Time: Prep 5 minutes; Cook 10 minutes

Per Serving:
Carbohydrate 29.5g
Protein 19.0g
Fat 1.8g
Fiber 1.4g
Cholesterol 37mg
Sodium 591mg
Calcium 51mg
Exchanges
2 Grain
2 Lean Meat

1	(11½-ounce) can vegetable juice
2	(5½-ounce) cans low-sodium vegetable juice
1	(11-ounce) can Mexican-style corn, drained
1	pound sole fillets cut into 1-inch pieces
2	tablespoons minced onion
2	teaspoons Worcestershire sauce
⅛	teaspoon ground red pepper
2	tablespoons minced fresh flat-leaf parsley
½	cup finely chopped green onions
6	(1-ounce) slices French bread

1 Combine first 7 ingredients in a large saucepan; bring to a boil over medium heat. Cover, reduce heat, and simmer 5 minutes or until fish flakes easily when tested with a fork, stirring occasionally.

2 Remove from heat; add parsley and green onions. Cover and let stand 5 minutes. Ladle into individual bowls. Serve with French bread slices.

Yield: 6 (1-cup) servings (215 calories per serving).

"For me, cooking is a creative endeavor. Experimenting with different foods and spices is an exciting adventure. It's the time when I can let my creative juices flow." — Jenny

Robust Vegetable Stew

Time: Prep 15 minutes; Cook 1 hour

1	(15-ounce) can garbanzo beans, drained
1	(14½-ounce) can no-salt-added whole tomatoes, undrained and chopped
2	cups peeled, cubed potato
2	cups diced carrot
1	cup sliced celery
½	cup dried lentils
½	cup finely chopped onion
2¼	cups water
1	(13¾-ounce) can no-salt-added beef broth, undiluted
¼	cup dry red wine
1	tablespoon low-sodium Worcestershire sauce
2	teaspoons chili powder
1	teaspoon ground cumin
½	teaspoon dried oregano
¼	teaspoon ground red pepper
½	cup plus 1 tablespoon (2¼ ounces) shredded 40% less-fat Cheddar cheese
	Chopped fresh cilantro (optional)

Per Serving:

Carbohydrate 31.2g
Protein 9.0g
Fat 2.2g
Fiber 4.6g
Cholesterol 4mg
Sodium 302mg
Calcium 108mg
Exchanges
1 Vegetable
1½ Grain
1 Lean Meat

1 Combine first 15 ingredients in a Dutch oven. Bring to a boil; cover, reduce heat, and simmer 1 hour or until lentils are tender.

2 Ladle stew into individual bowls; sprinkle each serving with 1 tablespoon cheese. Garnish with fresh cilantro, if desired.

Yield: 9 (1-cup) servings (174 calories per serving).

Mock Muffaletta

Time: Prep 15 minutes; Chill at least 2 hours

3   cups finely shredded romaine lettuce
½   small purple onion, thinly sliced and separated into rings
¼   cup crumbled blue cheese
3   tablespoons commercial oil-free Italian dressing
1   tablespoon red wine vinegar
1   tablespoon water
4   (2-ounce) submarine rolls, split
2   plum tomatoes, thinly sliced
½   teaspoon coarsely ground pepper
6   ounces thinly sliced cooked roast beef

1 Combine first 6 ingredients in a bowl; toss well.

2 Spoon lettuce mixture onto bottom halves of rolls. Top with tomato slices; sprinkle with pepper. Arrange roast beef over tomato. Top with remaining roll halves. Wrap in aluminum foil; chill at least 2 hours.

Yield: 4 servings (294 calories per serving).

Niçoise Loaf

Time: Prep 20 minutes; Chill up to 8 hours

1   (7-ounce) jar roasted red peppers in water
1   (16-ounce) round loaf sourdough bread
8   large basil leaves
2   (6⅛-ounce) cans 60%-less-salt tuna in water, drained
1   tablespoon balsamic vinegar
4   thin slices purple onion, separated into rings
4   canned artichoke hearts, drained and quartered
¼   cup sliced ripe olives
8   thin slices plum tomato

1 Drain peppers, discarding liquid. Dice peppers, and set aside.

2 Slice bread in half horizontally. Hollow out center of each half, leaving 1-inch-thick shells. Reserve inside of bread for another use.

3 Place basil leaves over bottom half of bread. Combine tuna and vinegar; toss well. Spoon over basil leaves. Top with diced pepper, onion, and remaining ingredients. Top with remaining bread half.

4 Wrap sandwich in heavy-duty plastic wrap. Place a pan holding 2 or 3 (1-pound) cans on top of sandwich to flatten, and refrigerate up to 8 hours. To serve, slice sandwich into 6 wedges.

Yield: 6 servings (238 calories per serving).

Niçoise Loaf

Fruit and Cheese Subs

Fruit and Cheese Subs

Time: Prep 20 minutes

Per Serving:
Carbohydrate 30.7g
Protein 13.0g
Fat 6.0g
Fiber 2.5g
Cholesterol 17mg
Sodium 563mg
Calcium 306mg
Exchanges
½ Fruit
1½ Grain
1 Medium-Fat Meat

¾ cup plus 2 tablespoons nonfat herb-and-garlic cream cheese, divided
1 tablespoon minced fresh dillweed
1 tablespoon commercial nonfat creamy cucumber dressing
1 cup peeled, finely chopped fresh peaches
1 cup seeded, finely chopped cucumber
3 tablespoons chopped almonds, toasted
1 (16-ounce) loaf Italian bread
6 green leaf lettuce leaves
5 ounces reduced-fat Havarti cheese, thinly sliced

1 Combine ¼ cup cream cheese, dillweed, and dressing. Add peaches, cucumber, and almonds; stir well.

2 Slice bread in half horizontally. Hollow out center of each half, leaving 1-inch-thick shells. Reserve inside of bread for another use.

3 Spread remaining ½ cup plus 2 tablespoons cream cheese over cut sides of bread. Place lettuce leaves on bottom half of bread. Spoon peach mixture over lettuce. Place cheese slices over peach mixture, and top with remaining bread half. Cut loaf into 8 slices.

Yield: 8 servings (229 calories per serving).

Open-Face Pepper-and-Cheese Melts

Time: Prep 18 minutes; Cook 2 minutes

Vegetable cooking spray
1   cup green pepper strips
1   tablespoon minced fresh basil
1   medium onion, sliced and separated into rings
1   clove garlic, minced
1   tablespoon plus 1 teaspoon stoneground mustard
4   (1-ounce) slices rye bread, toasted
8   (¼-inch-thick) slices unpeeled tomato (about 2 medium)
4   (1-ounce) slices part-skim mozzarella cheese, each cut lengthwise into
        4 strips

Per Serving:
Carbohydrate 26.6g
Protein 10.2g
Fat 7.4g
Fiber 3.5g
Cholesterol 22mg
Sodium 346mg
Calcium 187mg
Exchanges
2 Vegetable
1 Grain
1 Medium-Fat Meat

1 Coat a nonstick skillet with cooking spray; place over medium heat until hot. Add green pepper and next 3 ingredients; sauté 8 minutes or until tender. Set aside, and keep warm.

2 Spread 1 teaspoon mustard over each bread slice; place bread on a baking sheet. Top each with 2 slices tomato and 4 strips cheese. Broil 5½ inches from heat (with electric oven door partially opened) until cheese melts. Top evenly with green pepper mixture.

Yield: 4 servings (205 calories per serving).

Caesar Steak Sandwiches

Caesar Steak Sandwiches

Time: Prep 10 minutes; Stand 1 hour; Chill 2 hours

<table>
<tr><td>Per Serving:</td><td>1</td><td>(14-inch-diameter) round lavash (Armenian cracker bread)</td></tr>
<tr><td>Carbohydrate 15.3g</td><td>½</td><td>(8-ounce) package light process cream cheese</td></tr>
<tr><td>Protein 13.7g</td><td>2</td><td>tablespoons grated Parmesan cheese</td></tr>
<tr><td>Fat 7.9g</td><td>1</td><td>tablespoon lemon juice</td></tr>
<tr><td>Fiber 0.3g</td><td>1</td><td>tablespoon skim milk</td></tr>
<tr><td>Cholesterol 12mg</td><td>1</td><td>teaspoon low-sodium Worcestershire sauce</td></tr>
<tr><td>Sodium 541mg</td><td>½</td><td>teaspoon salt-free lemon-pepper seasoning</td></tr>
<tr><td>Calcium 68mg</td><td>¼</td><td>teaspoon garlic powder</td></tr>
<tr><td>Exchanges</td><td>½</td><td>pound thinly sliced cooked roast beef</td></tr>
<tr><td>1 Grain</td><td>12</td><td>romaine lettuce leaves</td></tr>
<tr><td>2 Lean Meat</td><td></td><td>Fresh watercress sprigs (optional)</td></tr>
</table>

1 Hold bread under a gentle spray of cold water for 10 seconds on each side or until moistened. Place between damp towels. Let stand 1 hour or until bread is soft and pliable. (If bread seems crisp in spots, sprinkle with more water.)

2 Beat cream cheese in a small bowl at medium speed of an electric mixer until smooth. Add Parmesan cheese and next 5 ingredients; stir well. Spread mixture on softened bread. Top with roast beef and lettuce leaves.

3 Roll up bread jellyroll fashion. Cover tightly with plastic wrap, and chill 2 hours. Cut roll into 6 slices. Garnish with fresh watercress, if desired.

Yield: 6 servings (186 calories per serving).

Southwestern Chicken Salad Sandwiches

Time: Prep 20 minutes

4	ounces nonfat cream cheese, softened
⅓	cup nonfat sour cream
2	tablespoons commercial no-salt-added mild salsa
½	teaspoon ground cumin
¼	teaspoon salt
¼	teaspoon ground red pepper
1½	cups shredded cooked chicken
⅓	cup finely chopped sweet red pepper
⅓	cup minced green onions
8	(¾-ounce) slices reduced-calorie whole wheat bread, toasted
16	medium-size fresh spinach leaves
1	cup alfalfa sprouts

Per Serving:
Carbohydrate 17.6g
Protein 25.3g
Fat 6.0g
Fiber 6.0g
Cholesterol 52mg
Sodium 595mg
Calcium 149mg
Exchanges
1 Vegetable
1 Grain
2 Lean Meat

1 Combine first 6 ingredients in a small bowl. Stir in chicken, chopped pepper, and green onions.

2 Spread evenly over 4 slices of bread; top with spinach leaves. Arrange alfalfa sprouts over spinach; top with remaining bread slices.

Yield: 4 servings (225 calories per serving).

Metric Conversions

Metric Measure/Conversion Chart

Approximate Conversion to Metric Measures

When You Know...	Multiply by... Mass (weight)	To Find...	Symbol
ounces	28	grams	g
pounds	0.45	kilograms	kg
	(volume)		
teaspoons	5	milliliters	ml
tablespoons	15	milliliters	ml
fluid ounces	30	milliliters	ml
cups	0.24	liters	l
pints	0.47	liters	l
quarts	0.95	liters	l

Cooking Measure Equivalents

Standard Cup	Volume (Liquid)	Liquid Solids (Butter)	Fine Powder (Flour)	Granular (Sugar)	Grain (Rice)
1	250 ml	200 g	140 g	190 g	150 g
¾	188 ml	150 g	105 g	143 g	113 g
⅔	167 ml	133 g	93 g	127 g	100 g
½	125 ml	100 g	70 g	95 g	75 g
⅓	83 ml	67 g	47 g	63 g	50 g
¼	63 ml	50 g	35 g	48 g	38 g
⅛	31 ml	25 g	18 g	24 g	19 g

Equivalent Measurements

3 teaspoons . . . . .1 tablespoon

4 tablespoons . . . . ¼ cup

5⅓ tablespoons . . . . ⅓ cup

8 tablespoons . . . . ½ cup

16 tablespoons . . . . 1 cup

2 tablespoons (liquid) . .1 ounce

1 cup . . . . .8 fluid ounces

2 cups . . . . .1 pint (16 fluid ounces)

4 cups . . . . .1 quart

4 quarts . . . . .1 gallon

⅛ cup . . . . .2 tablespoons

⅓ cup . . . . .5 tablespoons plus 1 teaspoon

⅔ cup . . . . .10 tablespoons plus 2 teaspoons

¾ cup . . . . .12 tablespoons

Recipe Index

Subject Index

Acknowledgments

I want to express my sincere and heartfelt thanks to the following people for their invaluable contributions and support in the development of my first-ever cookbook.

To my husband, Sid, for always encouraging me to go forward.

To Joe LaBonté and Jan Strode of *Jenny Craig International* and to Dianne Mooney of *Oxmoor House* who had the vision and determination to make this book a reality.

To the *Oxmoor House* test-kitchen staff, for their long hours and impeccable judgment in preparing and taste-testing the recipes in this book: Kathleen Phillips, Gayle Sadler, and their team of home economists (Molly Baldwin, Susan Bellows, Julie Christopher, Iris Crawley, Michelle Fuller, Natalie King, and Elizabeth Luckett). And special thanks to Jan Smith for helping to streamline so many of my family favorites.

To my editor, Cathy Wesler, R.D., whose sound and sensible creative approach to good food and nutrition mirrors my own personal philosophy.

To Lisa Talamini Jones, R.D., of *Jenny Craig International,* who worked with such diligence to assure that my own philosophies on lifestyle and nutrition melded perfectly with my publisher's culinary expertise.

Also, special thanks to Jim Bathie and Ralph Anderson, whose extraordinary photography in Del Mar and in the *Oxmoor House* studios grace the pages of this book. Thanks too for additional photography from Van Chaplin, Gary Clark, Tina Evans, Beth Maynor, Lee Puckett, and Charles Walton IV. And to my neighbor, Ron Fowler, for being gracious enough to lend us his lovely kitchen.

To Kay Clarke and Virginia Cravens, food stylists, whose artistic flair and discerning eye have shown our delicious recipes in their very best light. Thanks too for additional styling from Cindy Barr, Marjorie Johnson, and Cathy Muir.

To Melissa Clark whose talent with book design is evident on every page of this book. And to Rick Tucker for technical support and especially to James Boone for his superb art direction.

To Georgia Leonard, Brian Luscomb, Donna LaBonté, and Daren Drachman for their valuable insight during the planning of this book.

And finally, my gratitude to all my friends at *Oxmoor House* for their extraordinary professionalism: Nancy Wyatt, Kathy Eakin, and Olivia Wells, along with Shari Wimberly, Valorie Cooper, and Stacey Geary.